PostgreSQL Database Administration
Volume 1
Basic concepts

Federico Campoli

First edition, 2015, some rights reserved

License

Copyright

Preface

When I first came up with the idea to write a PostgreSQL DBA book, my intention was to publish it commercially.

Shortly I changed my mind as I became aware the uniqueness of a book for the database administrators. Then I decided to keep this book free. The same will happen for the next books in this series. I hope this will spread the knowledge on PostgreSQL becoming an useful reference.

Just a quick advice before you start reading. I beg your pardon in advance for my bad English. Unfortunately I'm not native English and it's very likely the book to be full of typos and bad grammar.

However, if you want to help me in cleaning and reviewing the text please to fork the github repository where I'm sharing the latex sources https://github.com/the4thdoctor/pgdba_books.

Intended audience

Database administrators, System administrators, Developers

Book structure

This book assumes the reader knows how to perform basic user operations such as connecting to the database and creating tables.

The book covers the basic aspects of database administration from installation to cluster management.

A couple of chapters are dedicated to the logical and physical structure in order to show both sides of coin. The triplet of maintenance backup and restore completes the the picture, not exhaustive but good enough to start getting "hands on" the product. The final chapter is dedicated to the developers. The various sections are giving advice that can seem quite obvious. But it's better to repeat things than having dangerous mistakes when building an application.

Version and platform

This book is based on PostgreSQL version 9.3 running on Debian GNU Linux 7. References to older versions or different platforms are explicitly specified.

Thanks

A big thank you to Craig Barnes for the priceless work on the book review.
The beautiful cover has been made by Chiaretta e Bon .

Contents

Chapter 1

PostgreSQL at a glance

PostgreSQL is a first class product with enterprise class features. This chapter is nothing but a general review on the product with a short section dedicated to the database's history.

1.1 Long time ago in a galaxy far far away...

Following the works of the Berkeley's Professor Michael Stonebraker, in 1996 Marc G. Fournier asked if there was volunteers interested in revamping the Postgres 95 project.

```
Date: Mon, 08 Jul 1996 22:12:19-0400 (EDT)
From: "Marc G. Fournier" <scrappy@ki.net>
Subject: [PG95]: Developers interested in improving PG95?
To: Postgres 95 Users <postgres95@oozoo.vnet.net>
Hi... A while back, there was talk of a TODO list and development moving forward on Postgres95 ...
at which point in time I volunteered to put up a cvs archive and sup server so that making updates
(and getting at the "newest source code") was easier to do...
... Just got the sup server up and running, and for those that are familiar with sup, the following
should work (ie. I can access the sup server from my machines using this):

. . . . . . . . . . . . . . . . . . . . . . . .
```

At this email replied Bruce Momjian,Thomas Lockhart, and Vadim Mikheev, the very first PostgreSQL Global Development Team.

Today, after almost 20 years and millions of rows of code, PostgreSQL is a robust and reliable relational database. The most advanced open source database. The slogan speaks truth indeed.

1.2   Features

Each time a new major release is released it adds new features to the already rich feature's set. What follows is a small excerpt of the latest PostgreSQL's version capabilities.

1.2.1   ACID compliant

The word ACID is an acronym for Atomicity, Consistency, Isolation and Durability. An ACID compliant database ensures those ules are enforced at any time.

- The atomiticy is enforced when a transaction is "all or nothing". For example if a transaction inserts a group of new rows. If just one row violates the primary key then the entire transaction must be rolled back leaving the table as nothing happened.

- The consistency ensures the database is constantly in a valid state. The database steps from a valid state to another valid state without exceptions.

- The isolation is enforced when the database status can be reached like all the concurrent transactions were run in serial.

- The durability ensures the committed transactions are saved on durable storage. In the event of the database crash the database must recover to last valid state.

1.2.2   MVCC

PostgreSQL ensures atomiticy consistency and isolation via the MVCC. The acronym stands for Multi Version Concurrency Control. The mechanism is incredibly efficient, it offers great level of concurrency keeping the transaction's snapshots isolated and consistent. There is one single disadvantage in the implementation. We'll see in detail in 7.6 how MVCC works and the reason why there's no such thing like an update in PostgreSQL.

1.2.3   Write ahead logging

The durability is implemented in PostgreSQL using the write ahead log. In short, when a data page is updated in the volatile memory the change is saved immediately on a durable location, the write ahead log. The page is written on the corresponding data file later. In the event of the database crash the write ahead log is scanned and all the not consistent pages are replayed on the data files. Each segment size is usually 16 MB and their presence is automatically managed by PostgreSQL. The write happens in sequence from the segment's top to the bottom. When this is full PostgreSQL switches to a new one. When this happens there is a log switch.

1.2.4 Point in time recovery

When PostgreSQL switches to a new WAL this could be a new segment or a recycled one. If the old WAL is archived in a safe location it's possible to get a copy of the physical data files meanwhile the database is running. The hot copy, alongside with the archived WAL segments have all the informations necessary and sufficient to recover the database's consistent state. The recovery by default terminates when all the archived data files are replayed. Anyway it's possible to stop the recover at a given point in time.

1.2.5 Standby server and high availability

The standby server is a database configured to stay in continuous recovery. This way a new archived WAL file is replayed as soon as it becomes available. This feature was first in introduced with PostgreSQL 8.4 as warm standby. From the version 9.0 PostgreSQL can be configured also in hot standby which allows the connections for read only queries.

1.2.6 Streaming replication

The WAL archiving doesn't work in real time. The segment is shipped only after a log switch and in a low activity server this can leave the standby behind the master for a while. It's possible to limit the problem using the archive_timeout parameter which forces a log swith after the given number of seconds. However, using the streaming replication a standby server can get the wal blocks over a database connection in almost real time. This feature allows the physical blocks to be transmitted over a conventional database connection.

1.2.7 Procedural languages

PostgreSQL have many procedural languages. Alongside with the pl/pgsql it's possible to write the procedure in many other popular languages like pl/perl and pl/python. From the version 9.1 is also supported the anonymous function's code block with the DO keyword.

1.2.8 Partitioning

Despite the partitioning implementation in PostgreSQL is still very basic it's not complicated to build an efficient partitioned structure using the table inheritance.

Unfortunately because the physical storage is distinct for each partition, is not possible to have a global primary key for the partitioned structure. The foreign keys can be emulated in some way using the triggers.

1.2.9 Cost based optimiser

The cost based optimiser, or CBO, is one of the PostgreSQL's point of strength The execution plan is dynamically determined from the data distribution and from the query parameters. PostgreSQL also supports the genetic query optimizer GEQO.

1.2.10 Multi platform support

PostgreSQL supports almost any unix flavour, and from version 8.0 runs natively on Windows.

1.2.11 Tablespaces

The tablespace support permits a fine grained distribution of the data files across filesystems. In 5.7 and 7.5 we'll see how to take advantage of this powerful feature.

1.2.12 Triggers

The triggers are well supported on tables and views. A basic implementation of the events triggers is also present. The triggers can emulate completely the updatable views feature.

1.2.13 Views

The read only views are well consodlidated in PostgreSQL. The version 9.3 introduced the basic support for the materialised and updatable views. For the materialised views there is no incremental refresh. The complex views, like views joining two or more tables, are not updatable.

1.2.14 Constraint enforcement

PostgreSQL supports primary keys and unique keys to enforce table's data. The referential integrity is guaranteed with the foreign keys. We'll take a look to the data integrity in 6

1.2.15 Extension system

PostgreSQL from the version 9.1 implements a very efficient extension system. The command CREATE EXTENSION makes the new features installation easy.

1.2.16 Federated

From PostgreSQL 9.1 is possible to have foreign tables pointing to external data sources. PostgreSQL 9.3 introduced also the foreign table's write the PostgreSQL's foreign data wrapper.

Chapter 2

Database installation

In this chapter will see how to install PostgreSQL on Debian Gnu Linux. We'll take a look to two procedures, compiling from source and using the packages shipped by the pgdg apt repository.

There are advantages and disadvantages on both procedures. The compile from source offers a fine grain control on all the aspects of the binaries configuration. Also doesn't have risks of unwanted restarts when upgrading and it's possible to install and upgrade the binaries with normal privileges.

The packaged install is easier to manage when deploying the new binaries on the server, in particular if there is a large number of installations to manage. The binary packages are released shortly after a new update is released. Because the frequency for the minor releases is not fixed, it could happen to have in place bugs affecting the production for months. For example the bug causing the standby server crashing when the master found invalid pages during a conventional vacuum, it was fixed almost immediately. Unfortunately the release with the fix appeared after five months.

2.1 Install from source

Using the configure script with the default settings requires the root access when installing. That's because the permissions in the target location /usr/local don't allow the write for normal users. This method adopts a different install location and requires the root access only for the os user creation and the dependencies install. Before starting the PostgreSQL part ask your sysadmin to run the following commands.

- useradd -d /home/postgres -s /bin/bash -m -U postgres

- passwd postgres

- apt-get update

- apt-get install build-essential libreadline6-dev zlib1g-dev

Please note the second step will require inserting a new user password. Unless is a personal test it's better to avoid obvious passwords like *postgres*.

In order to build the binaries we must download and extract the PostgreSQL's source tarball.

```
mkdir ~/download
cd ~/download
wget http://ftp.postgresql.org/pub/source/v9.3.5/postgresql-9.3.5.tar.bz2
tar xfj postgresql-9.3.5.tar.bz2
cd postgresql-9.3.5
```

Using the configure script's option –prefix we'll point the install directory to a writable location. We can also use a director named after the the major version's numbering. This will allow us to have installed different PostgreSQL versions without problems.

```
mkdir -p /home/postgres/bin/9.3
./configure --prefix=/home/postgres/bin/9.3
```

The configuration script will check all the dependencies and, if there's no error, will generate the makefiles. Then we can start the build simply running the command *make*. The time required for compiling is variable and depends from the system's power. If you have a multicore processor the make -j option can improve significantly the build time. When the build is is complete it's a good idea to to run the regression tests. Those tests are designed to find any regression or malfunction before the binaries are installed.

```
make
<very verbose output>

make check
```

The test's results are written in the source's subdirectory src/test/regress/results. If there's no error we can finalise the installation with the command make install.

```
make install
```

2.2 Packaged install

The PostgreSQL Global Development Group manages a repository in order to facilitate the installations on the Linux distributions based on the debian's packaging system.

Currently the supported distributions are

- Debian 6.0 (squeeze)

- Debian 7.0 (wheezy)

- Debian unstable (sid)

- Ubuntu 10.04 (lucid)

- Ubuntu 12.04 (precise)

- Ubuntu 13.10 (saucy)

- Ubuntu 14.04 (trusty)

The PostgreSQL's versions available are

- PostgreSQL 9.0

- PostgreSQL 9.1

- PostgreSQL 9.2

- PostgreSQL 9.3

- PostgreSQL 9.4

The he packages are available either for amd64 and i386 architecture.
Anyway, the up to date list is available on the the wiki page http://wiki.postgresql.org/wiki/Apt.

All the installation steps require root privileges, via sudo or acquiring the root login via
su. Before starting configuring the repository it's a good idea to import the GPG key for the
package validation.
In a root shell simply run

```
wget --quiet -O - https://www.postgresql.org/media/keys/ACCC4CF8.asc | sudo apt-key add -
```

When the key is imported create a file named pgdg.list into the directory /etc/apt/sources.d/
and add the following row.

```
deb http://apt.postgresql.org/pub/repos/apt/ {codename}-pgdg main
```

The distribution's codename can be found using the command lsb_release -c. e.g.

```
thedoctor@tardis:~$ lsb_release -c
Codename:       wheezy
```

After the repository configuration the installation is completed with two simple commands.

```
apt-get update
apt-get install postgreql-9.3 postgreql-contrib-9.3 postgreql-client-9.3
```

Be aware that this method, as automated installation task creates a new database cluster
in the default directory /var/lib/postgresql.

Chapter 3

Install structure

Depending on the installation method, the install structure is set up in a single directory or in multiple folders.

The install from source creates into the target directory four subfolders *bin include lib* and *share*.

- **bin** is the location for PostgreSQL's binaries

- **include** contains the server's header files

- **lib** is the location where to put the shared libraries

- **share** is where the example files and the extension configurations are stored

The packaged install puts the binaries and the libraries in the folder /usr/lib/postgresql organised by major version. For example the 9.3 install will put the binaries into /usr/lib/postgresql/9.3/bin and the libraries in /usr/lib/postgresql/9.3/lib. The extensions and contributed modules are installed into the folder /usr/share/postgresql with the same structure. In the directory /usr/bin/ are installed the debian's specific utilities and the symbolic link psql pointing the file /usr/lib/share/postgresql-common/pg_wrapper. This file is a perl script which calls the PostgreSQL client reading the version the cluster and the default database from the file /.postgresqlrc or in /etc/postgresql-common/user_clusters.

3.1 The core binaries

The PostgreSQL binaries can be split in two groups, the core and the wrappers alongside with the contributed modules. Let's start then with the former group.

3.1.1 postgres

This is the PostgreSQL's main process. The program can be started directly or using the pg_ctl utility. The second method is to be preferred as offer a simpler way to control the postgres process. The direct execution is the unavoidable choice when the database won't start for an old XID near to the wraparound failure. In this case the cluster can only start in single user mode to perform a cluster wide vacuum. For historical reasons there's also a symbolic link named postmaster pointing to the postgres executable.

3.1.2 pg_ctl

This utility is the simplest way for managing a PostgreSQL instance. The program reads the postgres pid from the cluster's data area and sending the os signals manages the start the stop or the process reload. It's also possible to send kill signals to the running instance. The pg_ctl The supported actions are the following.

- **init[db]** initialises a directory as PostgreSQL data area

- **start** starts a PostgreSQL instance

- **stop** shutdowns a PostgreSQL instance

- **reload** reloads the configuration's files

- **status** checks the PostgreSQL instance running status

- **promote** promotes a standby server

- **kill** sends a custom signal to the running instance

In 4 we'll se how to manage the cluster.

3.1.3 initdb

Is the binary which initialises the PostgreSQL data area. The directory to initialise must be empty. Various options can be specified on the command line, like the character enconding or the collation order.

3.1.4 psql

This is the PostgreSQL command line client. The client it looks very essential, however is one of the most flexible tools available to interact with the server and the only choice when working on the command line.

3.1.5 pg_dump

This is the binary dedicated to the backup. Can produce consistent backups in various formats. The usage is described shown in 9.

3.1.6 pg_restore

This program is used to restore a database reading a binary dump like the custom or directory format. It's able to run the restore in multiple jobs in order to speed up the process. The usage is described in 10

3.1.7 pg_controldata

This program can query the cluster's control file where PostgreSQLstores critical informations for the cluster activity and reliability.

3.1.8 pg_resetxlog

If a WAL file becomes corrupted the cluster cannot perform a crash recovery. This lead to a not startable cluster in case of system crash. In this catastrophic scenario there's still a possibility to start the cluster. Using pg_resetxlog the cluster is cleared of any WAL file, the control file is initialised from scratch and the transaction's count is restarted.

The *tabula rasa* have a cost indeed. The cluster lose any reference between the transactions progression and the data files. The physical integrity is lost and any attempt to run queries which write data will results in corruption.

The PostgreSQL's documentation is absolutely clear on this point.

```
After running pg_resetxlog the database must start without user access,
the entire content must be dumped, the data directory must be dropped and recreated
from scratch using initdb and then the dump file can be restored using psql or pg_restore
```

3.2 Wrappers and contributed modules

The second group of binaries is composed by the contributions and the wrappers. The contributed modules add functions otherwise not available. The wrappers add command line functions already present as SQL statements. Someone will notice the lack of HA specific binaries like pg_receivexlog and pg_archivecleanup. They have been purposely skipped because beyond the scope of this book.

3.2.1 The create and drop utilities

The binaries with the prefix create and drop like, createdb createlang createuser and dropdb, droplang, dropuser, are wrappers for the corresponding SQL functions. Each program performs the creation and the drop action on the corresponding named object. For example createdb adds a database to the cluster and dropdb will drop the specified database.

3.2.2 clusterdb

This program performs a database wide cluster on the tables with clustered indices. The binary can run on a single table specified on the command line. In 8.4 we'll take a look to CLUSTER and VACUUM FULL.

3.2.3 reindexdb

The command does a database wide reindex. It's possible to run the command just on a table or index passing the relation's name on the command line. In 8.3 we'll take a good look to the index management.

3.2.4 vacuumdb

This binary is a wrapper for the VACUUM SQL command. This is the most important maintenance task and shouldn't be ignored. The program performs a database wide VACUUM if executed without a target relation. Alongside with a common vacuum it's possible to have the usage statistics updated on the same time.

3.2.5 vacuumlo

This binary will remove the orphaned large objects from the pg_largeobject system table. The pg_largeobject is used to store the binary objects bigger than the limit of 1GB imposed by the bytea data type. The limit for a large object it is 2 GB since the version 9.2. From the version 9.3 the limit was increased to 4 TB.

3.3 Debian's specific utilities

Finally let's take a look to the debian's specific utilities. They are a collection of perl scripts used to simplify the cluster's management. Their install location is /usr/bin mostly like symbolic links to the actual executable. We already mentioned one of them in the chapter's introduction, the psql pointing to the pg_wrapper PERL script.

3.3.1 pg_createcluster

This script adds a new PostgreSQL cluster with the given major version, if installed, and the given name. The script puts all the configurations in /etc/postgresql. Each major version have a dedicated directory under which is present a group of directories with the cluster's specific configuration files. If not specified the data directory is created into the folder /var/lib/postgresql. It's also possible to specify the options for initd.

3.3.2   pg_dropcluster

The program delete a PostgreSQL cluster created previously with pg_createcluster. The program will not drop a running cluster. If the dropped cluster have any tablespace those must be manually removed after the drop as the program doesn't follow the symbolic links.

3.3.3   pg_lscluster

Lists the clusters created with pg_createcluster.

3.3.4   pg_ctlcluster

The program manages the cluster in a similar way pg_ctl does. Before the version 9.2 this wrapper had a dangerous behaviour for the shutdown. The script did not offered a flexible way to provide the shutdown mode. More informations about the shutdown sequence are in 4.3. Without any option pg_ctlcluster performs a smart shutdown mode. The –force option tells the script to try a *fast* shutdown mode. Unfortunately if the database doesn't shutdown in a *reasonable time* the script performs an *immediate* shutdown. After another short wait, if the the instance is still up the script sends a *kill -9* to the postgres process. Because this kind of actions can result in data loss they should be made manually by the DBA. It's better to avoid the shutdown using pg_ctlcluster.

Chapter 4

Managing the cluster

A PostgreSQL cluster is made of two components. A physical location initialised as data area and the postgres process attached to a shared memory segment, the shared buffer. The debian's package's installation, automatically set up a fully functional PostgreSQL cluster in the directory /var/lib/postgresql. This is good because it's possible to explore the product immediately. However, it's not uncommon to find clusters used in production with the minimal default configuration's values, just because the binary installation does not make it clear what happens *under the bonnet*.

This chapter will explain how a PostgreSQL cluster works and how critical is its management.

4.1 Initialising the data directory

The data area is initialised by initdb. The program requires an empty directory to write into to successful complete. Where the initdb binary is located depends from the installation method. We already discussed of this in 3 and 2.

The accepted parameters for customising cluster's data area are various. Anyway, running initdb without parameters will make the program to use the value stored into the environment variable PGDATA. If the variable is unset the program will exit without any further action.

For example, using the initdb shipped with the debian archive requires the following commands.

```
postgres@tardis:~/$ mkdir tempdata
postgres@tardis:~/$ cd tempdata
postgres@tardis:~/tempdata$ export PGDATA=`pwd`
postgres@tardis:~/tempdata$ /usr/lib/postgresql/9.3/bin/initdb
The files belonging to this database system will be owned by user "postgres".
This user must also own the server process.
```

```
The database cluster will be initialized with locale "en_GB.UTF-8".
The default database encoding has accordingly been set to "UTF8".
The default text search configuration will be set to "english".

Data page checksums are disabled.

fixing permissions on existing directory /var/lib/postgresql/tempdata ... ok
creating subdirectories ... ok
selecting default max_connections ... 100
selecting default shared_buffers ... 128MB
creating configuration files ... ok
creating template1 database in /var/lib/postgresql/tempdata/base/1 ... ok
initializing pg_authid ... ok
initializing dependencies ... ok
creating system views ... ok
loading system objects' descriptions ... ok
creating collations ... ok
creating conversions ... ok
creating dictionaries ... ok
setting privileges on built-in objects ... ok
creating information schema ... ok
loading PL/pgSQL server-side language ... ok
vacuuming database template1 ... ok
copying template1 to template0 ... ok
copying template1 to postgres ... ok
syncing data to disk ... ok

WARNING: enabling "trust" authentication for local connections
You can change this by editing pg_hba.conf or using the option -A, or
--auth-local and --auth-host, the next time you run initdb.

Success. You can now start the database server using:

    /usr/lib/postgresql/9.3/bin/postgres -D /var/lib/postgresql/tempdata
or
    /usr/lib/postgresql/9.3/bin/pg_ctl -D /var/lib/postgresql/tempdata -l
logfile start
```

PostgreSQL 9.3 introduces the data page checksums used for detecting the data page corruption. This great feature can be enabled only when initialising the data area with initdb and is cluster wide. The extra overhead caused by the checksums is something to consider because the only way to disable the data checksums is a dump and reload on a fresh data area.

After initialising the data directory initdb emits the message with the commands to start the database cluster. The first form is useful for debugging and development purposes because it starts the database directly from the command line with the output displayed on the terminal.

```
postgres@tardis:~/tempdata$ /usr/lib/postgresql/9.3/bin/postgres -D
/var/lib/postgresql/tempdata
LOG:  database system was shut down at 2014-03-23 18:52:07 UTC
LOG:  database system is ready to accept connections
LOG:  autovacuum launcher started
```

Pressing CTRL+C stops the cluster with a fast shutdown.

Starting the cluster with pg_ctl usage is very simple. This program also accepts the data area as parameter or using the environment variable PGDATA. It's also required to provide the command to execute. The start command for example is used to start the cluster in multi user mode.

```
postgres@tardis:~/tempdata$ /usr/lib/postgresql/9.3/bin/pg_ctl -D
/var/lib/postgresql/tempdata -l logfile start
server starting

postgres@tardis:~/tempdata$ tail logfile
LOG:  database system was shut down at 2014-03-23 19:01:19 UTC
LOG:  database system is ready to accept connections
LOG:  autovacuum launcher started
```

Omitting the logfile with the -l will display the alerts and warnings on the terminal.
The command stop will end the cluster's activity.

```
postgres@tardis:~$ /usr/lib/postgresql/9.3/bin/pg_ctl -D
/var/lib/postgresql/tempdata -l logfile stop
waiting for server to shut down.... done
server stopped
```

4.2 The startup sequence

When PostgreSQL starts the server process then the shared memory is allocated. Before the version 9.3 this was often cause of trouble because the default kernel's limits. An error like this it means the requested amount of memory is not allowed by the OS settings.

```
FATAL: could not create shared memory segment: Cannot allocate memory
```

```
DETAIL: Failed system call was shmget(key=X, size=XXXXXX, XXXXX).
```

```
HINT: This error usually means that PostgreSQL's request for a shared memory
segment exceeded available memory or swap space, or exceeded your kernel's
SHMALL parameter. You can either reduce the request size or reconfigure the
kernel with larger SHMALL. To reduce the request size (currently XXXXX bytes),
reduce PostgreSQL's shared memory usage, perhaps by reducing shared_buffers or
max_connections.
```

The kernel parameter governing this limit is SHMMAX, the maximum size of shared
memory segment. The value is measured in bytes and must be bigger than the shared_buffers
parameter. Another parameter which needs adjustment is SHMALL. This value sets the
amount of shared memory available and usually on linux is measured in pages. Unless the
kernel is configured to allow the huge pages the page size is 4096 byes. The value should be
the same as SHMMAX. Changing those parameters requires the root privileges. It's a good
measure to have a small extra headroom for the needed memory instead of setting the exact
require value.

For example, setting the shared buffer to 1 GB requires SHMMAX to be at least 1073741824.
The value 1258291200 (1200 MB) is a reasonable setting. The corresponding SHMALL is
307200. The value SHMMNI is the minimum value of shared memory, is safe to set to 4096,
one memory page.

```
kernel.shmmax = 1258291200
kernel.shmall = 307200
kernel.shmmni = 4096
kernel.sem = 250 32000 100 128
fs.file-max = 658576
```

To apply the changes login as root and run *sysctl -p*.

When the memory is allocated the postmaster reads the pg_control file to check if the
instance requires recovery. The pg_control file is used to store the locations to the last checkpoint and the last known status for the instance.

If the instance is in dirty state, because a crash or an unclean shutdown, the startup process reads the last checkpoint location and replays the blocks from the corresponding WAL
segment in the pg_xlog directory. Any corruption in the wal files during the recovery or the
pg_control file results in a not startable instance.

When the recovery is complete or if the cluster's state is clean the postgres process completes the startup and sets the cluster in production state.

4.3   The shutdown sequence

The PostgreSQL process enters the shutdown status when a specific OS signal is received. The signal can be sent via the os kill or using the program pg_ctl.

As seen in 3.1.2 pg_ctl accepts the -m switch when the command is stop. The -m switch is used to specify the shutdown mode and if is omitted it defaults to smart which corresponds to the SIGTERM signal. With the smart shuthdown the cluster stops accepting new connections and waits for all backends to quit.

When the shutdown mode is set to fast pg_ctl sends the SIGINT signal to the postgres main process. Like the smart shutdown the cluster does not accepts new connections and terminates the existing backends. Any open transaction is rolled back.

When the smart and the fast shutdown are complete they leave the cluster in clean state. This is true because when the postgres process initiate the final part of the shutdown it starts a last checkpoint which consolidates any dirty block on the disk. Before quitting the postgres process saves the latest checkpoint's location to the pg_control file and marks the cluster as clean.

The checkpoint can slow down the entire shutdown sequence. In particular if the shared_buffer is big and contains many dirty blocks, the checkpoint can run for a very long time. Also if at the shutdown time, another checkpoint is running the postgres process will wait for this checkpoint to complete before starting the final checkpoint.

Enabling the log checkpoints in the configuration gives us some visibility on what the cluster is actually doing. The GUC parameter governing the setting is log_checkpoints.

If the cluster doesn't stop, there is a shutdown mode which leaves the cluster in dirty state. The immiediate shutdown. The equivalent signal is the SIGQUIT and it causes the main process alongside with the backends to quit immediately without the checkpoint.

The subsequent start will require a crash recovery. The recovery is usually harmless with one important exception. If the cluster contains unlogged tables those relations are recreated from scratch when the recovery happens and all the data in those table is lost.

A final word about the SIGKILL signal, the dreaded kill -9. It could happen the cluster will not stop even using the immediate mode. In this case, the last resort is to use SIGKILL. Because this signal cannot be trapped in any way, the resources like the shared memory and the inter process semaphores will stay in place after killing the server. This will very likely affect the start of a fresh instance. Please refer to your sysadmin to find out the best way to cleanup the memory after the SIGKILL.

4.4 The processes

Alongside with postgres process there are a number of accessory processes. With a running 9.3 cluster ps shows at least six postgres processes.

4.4.1 postgres: checkpointer process

As the name suggests this process take care of the cluster's checkpoint activity. A checkpoint is an important event in the cluster's life. When it starts all the dirty pages in memory are written to the data files. The checkpoint frequency is regulated by the time and the number of cluster's WAL switches.The GUC parameters governing this metrics are respectively checkpoint_timeout and checkpoint_segments. There is a third parameter, the checkpoint_completion_target which sets the percentage of the checkpoint_timeout. The cluster uses this value to spread the checkpoint over this time in order to avoid a big disk IO spike.

4.4.2 postgres: writer process

The background writer scans the shared buffer searching for dirty pages which writes on the data files. The process is designed to have a minimal impact on the database activity. It's possible to tune the length of a run and the delay between the writer's runs using the GUC parameters bgwriter_lru_maxpages and bgwriter_delay. They are respectively the number of dirty buffers written before the writer's sleep and the time between two runs.

4.4.3 postgres: wal writer process

This background process has been introduced with the 9.3 in order to make the WAL writes a more efficient. The process works in rounds and writes down the wal buffers to the wal files. The GUC parameter wal_writer_delay sets the milliseconds to sleep between the rounds.

4.4.4 postgres: autovacuum launcher process

This process is present if the autovacuum is enabled. It's purpose is to launch the autovacuum backends when needed.

4.4.5 postgres: stats collector process

The process gathers the database's usage statistics and stores the information to the location indicated by the GUC stats_temp_directory. This is by default pg_stat_temp, a relative path to the data area.

4.4.6 postgres: postgres postgres [local] idle

This is a database backend. There is one backend for each established connection. The values after the colon show useful information. In particular between the square brackets there is the query the backend is executing.

4.5   The memory

Externally the PostgreSQL's memory structure is very simple to understand. Alongside with a single shared segment there are the per user memories. Behind the scenes things are quite complex and beyond the scope of this book.

4.5.1   The shared buffer

The shared buffer, as the name suggests is the segment of shared memory used by PostgreSQL to manage the data pages shared across the backends. The shared buffer's size is set using the GUC parameter shared_buffers. Any change requires the cluster's restart.

The memory segment is formatted in pages like the data files. When a new backend is forked from the main process is attached to the shared buffer. Because usually the shared buffer is a fraction of the cluster's size, a simple but very efficient mechanism keeps in memory the blocks using a combination of LRU and MRU. Since the version 8.3 is also present a protection mechanism against the page eviction from the memeory in the case of IO intensive operations.

Any data operation is performed loading the data pages in the shared buffer. Alongside with the benefits of the memory cache there is the enforcement of the data consistency at any time.

In particular, if any backend crash happens PostgreSQL resets all the existing connections to protect the shared buffer from potential corruption.

4.5.2   The work memory

The work memory is allocated for each connected session. Its size is set using the GUC parameter work_mem. The value can be set just for the current session using the SET statement or globally in the postgresql.conf file.In this case the change becomes effective immediately after the cluster reloads the configuration file.

A correct size for this memory can improve the performance of any memory intensive operation like the sorts. It's very important to set this value to a reasonable size in order to avoid any risk of out of memory error or unwanted swap.

4.5.3   The maintenance work memory

The maintenance work memory is set with the parameter maintenance_work_mem and like the work_mem is allocated for each connected session. PostgreSQL uses this memory in the maintenance operations like VACUUM or REINDEX. The value can be bigger than work_mem. In 8.1 there are more information about it. The maintenance_work_mem value can be set on the session or globally like the work memory.

4.5.4 The temporary memory

The temporary memory is set using the parameter temp_buffers. The main usage is for storing the the temporary tables. If the table doesn't fit in the allocated memory then the relation is saved on on disk. It's possible to change the temp_buffers value for the current session but only before creating a temporary table.

4.6 The data area

As seen in 4.1 the data area is initialised using initdb . In this section we'll take a look to some of the PGDATA's sub directories.

4.6.1 base

This directory it does what the name suggests. It holds the database files. For each database in the cluster there is a dedicated sub directory in base named after the database's object id. A new installation shows only three sub directories in the base folder.

Two of them are the template databases,template0 and template1. The third is the postgres database. In 5 there are more information about the logical structure.

Each database directory contains many files with the numerical names. They are the physical database's files, tables indices etc.

The relation's file name is set initially using the relation's object id. Because there are operations that can change the file name (e.g. VACUUM FULL, REINDEX) PostgreSQL tracks the file name in a different pg_class's field, the relfilenode. In 7 there are more information about the physical data file structure.

4.6.2 global

The global directory holds all the shared relations. Alongside with the data files there is a small file, just one data page, called pg_control. This file is vital for the cluster's activity . If there is any corruption on the control file the cluster cannot start.

4.6.3 pg_xlog

This is probably the most important and critical directory in the data area. The directory holds the write ahead logs, also known as WAL files. Each segment is by default 16 MB and is used to store the records for the pages changed in the shared buffer. The write first on on this durable storage ensures the cluster's crash recovery. In the event of a crash the WAL are replayed when the startup begins from the last checkpoint location read from control file.Because this directory is heavily written, putting it on a dedicated device improves the performance.

4.6.4   pg_clog

This directory contains the status of the committed transactions stored in many files, each one big like a data page. The directory does not store the status of the transactions executed with the SERIALIZABLE isolation. The directory is managed by PostgreSQL. The number of files is controlled by the two parameters autovacuum_freeze_max_age and vacuum_freeze_table_age. They control the "event horizon" of the oldest frozen transaction id and the pg_clog must store the commit status accordingly.

4.6.5   pg_serial

This directory is similar to the pg_clog except the commit statuses are only for the transactions executed with the SERIALIZABLE isolation level.

4.6.6   pg_multixact

The directory stores the statuses of the multi transactions. They are used in general for the row share locks.

4.6.7   pg_notify

The directory is used to stores the LISTEN/NOTIFY operations.

4.6.8   pg_snapshots

This directory stores the exported transaction's snapshots. From the version 9.2 PostgreSQL can export a consistent snapshot to the other sessions. More details about the snapshots are in 5.8.1.

4.6.9   pg_stat_tmp

This directory contains the temporary files generated by the statistic subsystem. Because the directory is constantly written, changing its location to a ramdisk can improve the performance. The parameter stats_temp_directory can be changed with a simple reload.

4.6.10   pg_stat

This directory contains the files saved permanently by the statistic subsystem to keep them persistent between the restarts.

4.6.11   pg_subtrans

In this folder there are the subtransactions statuses.

4.6.12 pg_twophase

There is where PostgreSQL saves the two phase commit's data. This feature allow a transaction to become independent from the backend status. If the backend disconnects, for example in a network outage, the transaction does not rollbacks waiting for another backend to pick it up and complete the commit.

4.6.13 pg_tblspc

In this folder there are the symbolic links to the tablespace locations. In 5.7 and 7.5 there are more informations about it.

Chapter 5

The logical layout

In this we'll take a look to the PostgreSQL logical layout. We'll start with the connection process. Then we'll see the logical relations like tables, indices and views. The chapter will end with the tablespaces and the MVCC.

5.1 The connection

When a client starts a connection to a running cluster, the process pass through few steps.

The first connection's stage is the check using the host based authentication. The cluster scans the pg_hba.conf file searching a match for the connection's parameters. Those are, for example, the client's host, the user etc. The host file is usually saved inside the the data area alongside the configuration file postgresql.conf. The pg_hba.conf is read from the top to the bottom and the first matching row for the client's parameters is used to determine the authentication method to use. If PostgreSQL reaches the end of the file without match the connection is refused.

The pg_hba.conf structure is shown in 5.1

Type	Database	User	Address	Method
local	name	name	ipaddress/network mask	trust
host	*	*	host name	reject
hostssl				md5
hostnossl				password
				gss
				sspi
				krb5
				ident
				peer
				pam
				ldap
				radius
				cert

Table 5.1: pg_hba.conf

The column type specifies if the connection is local or host. The former is when the connection is made using a socket. The latter when the connection uses the network. It's also possible to specify if the host connection should be secure or plain using hostssl and hostnossl.

The Database and User columns are used to match specific databases and users.

The column address have sense only if the connection is host, hostssl or hostnossl. The value can be an ip address plus the network mask. Is also possible to specify the hostname. There is the full support for ipv4 and ipv6.

The pg_hba.conf's last column is the authentication method for the matched row. The action to perform after the match is done. PostgreSQL supports many methods ranging from the plain password challenge to kerberos.

We'll now take a look to the built in methods.

- **trust**: The connection is authorised without any further action. Is quite useful if the password is lost. Use it with caution.

- **peer**: The connection is authorised if the OS user matches the database user. It's useful for the local connections.

- **password**: The connection establishes if the connection's user and the password matches with the values stored in the pg_shadow system table. This method sends the password in clear text. Should be used only on trusted networks.

- **md5**: This method is similar to password. It uses a better security encoding the passwords using the md5 algorithm. Because md5 is deterministic, there is pseudo random subroutine which prevents to have the same string sent over the network.

44

- **reject**: The connection is rejected. This method is very useful to keep the sessions out of the database. e.g. maintenance requiring single user mode.

When the connection establishes the postgres main process forks a new backend process attached to the shared buffer. The fork process is expensive. This makes the connection a potential bottleneck. Opening new connections can degrade the operating system performance and eventually produce zombie processes. Keeping the connections constantly connected maybe is a reasonable fix. Unfortunately this approach have a couple of unpleasant side effects.

Changing any connection related parameter like the max_connections, requires a cluster restart. For this reason planning the resources is absolutely vital. For each connection present in max_connections the cluster allocates 400 bytes of shared memory. For each connection established the cluster allocates a per user memory area wich size is determined by the parameter work_mem.

For example let's consider a cluster with a shared_buffer set to 512 MB and the work_mem set to 100MB. Setting the max_connections to only 500 requires a potentially 49 GB of total memory if all the connections are in use. Because the work_mem can affects the performances, its value should be determined carefully. Being a per user memory any change to work_mem does not require the cluster's start but a simple reload.

In this kind of situations a connection pooler can be a good solutions. The sophisticated pgpool or the lightweight pgbouncer can help to boost the connection's performance.

By default a fresh data area initialisation listens only on the localhost. The GUC parameter governing this aspect is listen_addresses. In order to have the cluster accepting connections from the rest of the network the values should change to the correct listening addresses specified as values separated by commas. It's also possible to set it to * as wildcard.
Changing the parameters max_connections and listen_addresses require the cluster restart.

5.2 Databases

Unlikely other DBMS, a PostgreSQL connection requires the database name in the connection string. Sometimes this can be omitted in psql when this information is supplied in another way.

When omitted psql checks if the environment variable $PGDATABASE is set. If $PGDATABASE is missing then psql defaults the database name to connection's username. This leads to confusing error messages. For example, if we have a username named test but not a database named test the connection will fail even with the correct credentials.

```
postgres@tardis:~$ psql -U test -h localhost
Password for user test:
```

```
psql: FATAL:  database "test" does not exist
```

This error appears because the pg_hba.conf allow the connection for any database. Even for a not existing one. The connection is then terminated when the backend ask to connect to the database named test which does not exists.

This is very common for the new users. The solution is incredibly simple because in a PostgreSQL cluster there are at least three databases. Passing the name template1 as last parameter will do the trick.

```
postgres@tardis:~$ psql -U test -h localhost template1
Password for user test:
psql (9.3.4)
SSL connection (cipher: DHE-RSA-AES256-SHA, bits: 256)
Type "help" for help.
```

When the connection is established we can query the system table pg_database to get the cluster's database list.

```
template1=> SELECT datname FROM pg_database;
   datname
---------------
 template1
 template0
 postgres
(3 rows)
```

Database administrators coming from other DBMS can be confused by the postgres database. This database have nothing special. Its creation was added since the version 8.4 because it was useful to have it. You can just ignore it or use it for testing purposes. Dropping the postgres database does not corrupts the cluster. Because this database is often used by third party tools before dropping it check if is in use in any way.

The databases template0 and template1 like the name suggests are the template databases. A template database is used to build new database copies via the physical file copy.

When initdb initialises the data area the database template1 is populated with the correct references to the WAL records, the system views and the procedural language PL/PgSQL. When this is done the database template0 and the postgres databases are then created using the template1 database.

The database template0 doesn't allow the connections. It's main usage is to rebuild the database template1 if it gets corrupted or for creating databases with a character encoding/ctype, different from the cluster wide settings.

```
postgres=# CREATE DATABASE db_test WITH ENCODING 'UTF8' LC_CTYPE 'en_US.UTF-8';
ERROR:  new LC_CTYPE (en_US.UTF-8) is incompatible with the LC_CTYPE of the
template database (en_GB.UTF-8)
HINT:  Use the same LC_CTYPE as in the template database, or use template0 as
template.
```

```
postgres=# CREATE DATABASE db_test WITH ENCODING 'UTF8' LC_CTYPE 'en_US.UTF-8'
TEMPLATE template0;
CREATE DATABASE
postgres=#
```

If the template is omitted the CREATE DATABASE statement will use template1 by default.

A database can be renamed or dropped with ALTER DATABASE and DROP DATABASE statements. Those operations require the exclusive access to the affected database. If there are connections established the drop or rename will fail.

```
postgres=# ALTER DATABASE db_test RENAME TO db_to_drop;
ALTER DATABASE

postgres=# DROP DATABASE db_to_drop;
DROP DATABASE
```

5.3   Tables

In our top down approach to the PostgreSQL's logical model, the next step is the relation. In the PostgreSQL jargon a relation is an object which carries the data or the way to retrieve the data. A relation can have a physical counterpart or be purely logical. We'll take a look in particular to three of them starting with the tables.

A table is the fundamental storage unit for the data. PostgreSQL implements many kind of tables with different levels of durability. A table is created using the SQL command CREATE TABLE. The data is stored into a table without any specific order. Because the MVCC implementation a row update can change the row's physical position. For more informations look to 7.6. PostgreSQL implements three kind of tables.

5.3.1   Logged tables

By default CREATE TABLE creates a logged table. This kind of table implements the durability logging any change to the write ahead log. The data pages are loaded in the shared buffer and any change to them is logged first to the WAL. The consolidation to the the data file happens later.

5.3.2   Unlogged tables

An unlogged table have the same structure like the logged table. The difference is such kind of tables are not crash safe. The data is still consolidated to the data file but the pages modified in memory do not write their changes to the WAL. The main advantage is the write operations which are considerably faster at the cost of the data durability. The data stored into an ulogged table should be considered partially volatile. The database will truncate those tables when the crash recovery occurs. Because the unlogged table don't write to the WAL, those tables are not accessible on a physical standby.

5.3.3 Temporary tables

A temporary table is a relation which lives into the backend's local memory. When the connection ends the table is dropped. Those table can have the same name for all the sessions because they are completely isolated. If the amount of data stored into the table is lesser than the temp_buffers value the table will fit in memory with great speed advantage. Otherwise the database will create a temporary relation on disk. The parameter temp_buffers can be altered for the session but only before the first temporary table is created.

5.3.4 Foreign tables

The foreign tables were first introduced with PostgreSQL 9.1 as read only relations, improving considerably the DBMS connectivity with other data sources. A foreign table works exactly like a local table. A foreign data wrapper interacts with the foreign data source and handles the data flow.

There are many different foreign data wrappers available for very exotic data sources. From the version 9.3 the postgres_fdw becomes available and the the foreign tables are writable. The implementation of the postgres_fdw implementation is similar to old dblink module with a more efficient performance management and the connection's caching.

5.4 Table inheritance

PostgreSQL is an Object Relational Database Management System rather a simple DBMS. Some of the concepts present in the object oriented programming are implemented in the PostgreSQL logic. The relations are also known as classes and the table's columns as attributes.

The table inheritance is a logical relationship between a parent table and one or more child tables. The child table inherits the parent's attribute structure but not the physical storage.

Creating a parent/child structure is straightforward.

```
db_test=#CREATE TABLE t_parent
                    (
                          i_id_data        integer,
                          v_data           character varying(300)
                    );

CREATE TABLE

db_test=#CREATE TABLE t_child_01

                    ()
             INHERITS (t_parent)
                    ;
```

```
db_test=# \d t_parent
            Table "public.t_parent"
  Column   |          Type          | Modifiers
-----------+------------------------+-----------
 i_id_data | integer                |
 v_data    | character varying(300) |
Number of child tables: 1 (Use \d+ to list them.)

db_test=# \d t_child_01
           Table "public.t_child_01"
  Column   |          Type          | Modifiers
-----------+------------------------+-----------
 i_id_data | integer                |
 v_data    | character varying(300) |
Inherits: t_parent
```

The inheritance is usually defined at creation time. It's possible to enforce the inheritance between two existing tables with the ALTER TABLE ... INHERIT command. The two table's structure must be identical.

```
db_test=# ALTER TABLE t_child_01 NO INHERIT t_parent;
ALTER TABLE
db_test=# ALTER TABLE t_child_01 INHERIT t_parent;
ALTER TABLE
```

Because the physical storage is not shared then the unique constraints aren't globally enforced on the inheritance tree. This prevents the creation of any global foreign key. Using the table inheritance, combined with the constraint exclusion and the triggers/rules, is a partial workaround for the table partitioning.

5.5   Indices

An index is a structured relation. The indexed entries are used to access the tuples stored in the tables. The index entries are the actual data with a pointer to the corresponding table's pages.

It's important to bear in mind that the indices add overhead to the write operations. Creating an index does not guarantee its usage. The cost based optimiser, for example, can simply consider the index access more expensive than a sequential access. The stats system views, like the pg_stat_all_indexes, store the usage counters for the indices.

For example this simple query finds all the indices in the public schema with index scan counter zero.

```
SELECT
        schemaname,
        relname,
        indexrelname,
        idx_scan
FROM
```

```
        pg_stat_all_indexes
WHERE
            schemaname='public'
        AND     idx_scan=0
;
```

Having an efficient maintenance plan can improve sensibly the database performance. Take a look to 8 for more information.

PostgreSQL implements many kind of indices. The keyword USING specifies the index type at create time.

```
CREATE INDEX idx_test ON t_test USING hash (t_contents);
```

If the clause USING is omitted the index defaults to the B-tree.

5.5.1 b-tree

The general purpose B-tree index implements the Lehman and Yao's high-concurrency B-tree management algorithm. The B-tree can handle equality and range queries returning ordered data. The indexed values are stored into the index pages with the pointers to the table's pages. Because the index is a relation not TOASTable the max length for an indexed key is 1/3 of the page size. More informations about TOAST are in 7.4

5.5.2 hash

The hash indices can handle only equality and are not WAL logged. Their changes are not replayed if the crash recovery occurs and do not propagate to the standby servers.

5.5.3 GiST

The GiST indices are the Generalised Search Tree. The GiST is a collection of indexing strategies organised under a common infrastructure. They can implement arbitrary indexing schemes like B-trees, R-trees or other. The default installation comes with operator classes working on two elements geometrical data and for the nearest-neighbour searches. The GiST indices do not perform an exact match. The false positives are removed with second rematch on the table's data.

5.5.4 GIN

The GIN indices are the Generalised Inverted Indices. This kind of index is optimised for indexing the composite data types, arrays and vectors like the full text search elements. This is the only index supported by the range types. The GIN are exact indices, when scanned the returned set doesn't require recheck.

5.6   Views

A view is a relation composed by a name and a query definition. This permits a faster access to complex SQL. When a view is created the query is validated and all the objects involved are translated to their binary representation. All the wildcards are expanded to the corresponding field's list.

A simple example will help us to understand better this important concept. Let's create a table populated using the function generate_series(). We'll then create a view with a simple SELECT * from the original table.

```
CREATE TABLE t_data
        (
                i_id              serial,
                t_content         text
        );

ALTER TABLE t_data
ADD CONSTRAINT pk_t_data PRIMARY KEY (i_id);


INSERT INTO t_data
        (
                t_content
        )
SELECT
        md5(i_counter::text)
FROM
        (
                SELECT
                        i_counter
                FROM
                        generate_series(1,200) as i_counter
        ) t_series;

CREATE OR REPLACE VIEW v_data
AS
  SELECT
        *
  FROM
        t_data;
```

We can select from the view and from the the table with a SELECT and get the same data. The view's definition in pg_views shows no wildcard though.

```
db_test=# \x
db_test=# SELECT * FROM pg_views where viewname='v_data';
-[ RECORD 1 ]--------------------
schemaname | public
viewname   | v_data
viewowner  | postgres
definition |   SELECT t_data.i_id,
```

```
|        t_data.t_content
|     FROM t_data;
```

If we add a new field to the table t_data this will not applies to the view.

```
ALTER TABLE t_data ADD COLUMN d_date date NOT NULL default now()::date;

db_test=# SELECT * FROM t_data LIMIT 1;
 i_id |              t_content              |   d_date
------+-------------------------------------+------------
    1 | c4ca4238a0b923820dcc509a6f75849b | 2014-05-21
(1 row)


db_test=# SELECT * FROM v_data LIMIT 1;
 i_id |              t_content
------+-------------------------------------
    1 | c4ca4238a0b923820dcc509a6f75849b
(1 row)
```

Using the statement CREATE OR REPLACE VIEW we can put the view in sync with the table's structure.

```
CREATE OR REPLACE VIEW v_data
AS
  SELECT
        *
  FROM
        t_data;

db_test=# SELECT * FROM v_data LIMIT 1;
 i_id |              t_content              |   d_date
------+-------------------------------------+------------
    1 | c4ca4238a0b923820dcc509a6f75849b | 2014-05-21
(1 row)
```

Using the wildcards in the queries is a bad practice for many reasons. The potential outdated match between the physical and the logical relations is one of those.

The way PostgreSQL implements the views guarantee they never invalidate when the referred objects are renamed.

If new attributes needs to be added to the view the CREATE OR REPLACE statement can be used but only if the fields are appended. If a table is referred by a view the drop is not possible. It's still possible to drop a table with all the associated views using the clause CASCADE. This is a dangerous practice though. The dependencies can be very complicated and a not careful drop can result in a regression. The best approach is to check for the dependencies using the table pg_depend.

Storing a complex SQL inside the database avoid the overhead caused by the round trip between the client and the server. A view can be joined with other tables or views. This practice is generally bad because the planner can be confused by mixing different queries and can generate not efficient execution plans.

A good system to spot a view when writing a query is to use a naming convention. For example adding a v_ in the view names and the t_ in the table names will help the database developer to avoid mixing logical an physical objects when writing SQL. Look to 11 for more information.

PostgreSQL from the version 9.3 supports the updatable views. This feature is limited just to the simple views. A view is defined simple when the following is true.

- Does have exactly one entry in its FROM list, which must be a table or another updatable view.

- Does not contain WITH, DISTINCT, GROUP BY, HAVING,LIMIT, or OFFSET clauses at the top level.

- Does not contain set operations (UNION, INTERSECT or EXCEPT) at the top level

- All columns in the view's select list must be simple references to columns of the underlying relation. They cannot be expressions, literals or functions. System columns cannot be referenced, either.

- Columns of the underlying relation do not appear more than once in the view's select list.

- Does not have the security_barrier property.

A complex view can still become updatable using the triggers or the rules.

Another feature introduced by the 9.3 is the materialised views. This acts like a physical snapshot of the saved SQL. The view's data can be refreshed with the statement REFRESH MATERIALIZED VIEW.

5.7 Tablespaces

A tablespace is a logical name pointing to a physical location. This feature was introduced with the release 8.0 and its implementation did not change too much since then. From the version 9.2 a new function pg_tablespace_location(tablespace_oid) offers the dynamic resolution of the physical tablespace location,making the dba life easier.

When a new physical relation is created without tablespace indication, the value defaults to the parameter default_tablespace. If this parameter is not set then the relation's tablespace is set to the database's default tablespace. Into a fresh initialised cluster there are two tablespaces initially. One is the pg_default which points to the path $PGDATA/base. The second is pg_global which is reserved for the cluster's shared objects and its physical path is $PGDATA/global.

Creating a new tablespace is very simple. The physical location must be previously created and the os user running the postgres process shall be able to write into it. Let's create, for example, a tablespace pointing to the folder named /var/lib/postgresql/pg_tbs/ts_test. Our new tablespace will be named ts_test.

```
CREATE TABLESPACE ts_test
OWNER postgres
LOCATION '/var/lib/postgresql/pg_tbs/ts_test' ;
```

Only superusers can create tablespaces. The clause OWNER is optional and if is omitted the tablespace's owner defaults to the user issuing the command. The tablespaces are cluster wide and are listed into the pg_tablespace system table.

The clause TABLESPACE followed by the tablespace name will create the new relation into the specified tablespace.

```
CREATE TABLE t_ts_test
        (
                i_id serial ,
                v_value text
        )
TABLESPACE ts_test ;
```

A relation can be moved from a tablespace to another using the ALTER command. The following command moves the table t_ts_test from the tablespace ts_test to pg_default.

```
ALTER TABLE t_ts_test SET TABLESPACE pg_default;
```

The move is transaction safe but requires an access exclusive lock on the affected relation. The lock prevents accessing the relation's data for the time required by the move.If the relation have a significant size this could result in a prolonged time where the table's data is not accessible. The exclusive lock conflicts any running pg_dump which prevents any tablespace change.

A tablespace can be removed with DROP TABLESPACE command but must be empty before the drop. There's no CASCADE clause for the DROP TABLESPACE command.

```
postgres=# DROP TABLESPACE ts_test;
ERROR:  tablespace "ts_test" is not empty

postgres=# ALTER TABLE t_ts_test SET TABLESPACE pg_default;
ALTER TABLE
postgres=# DROP TABLESPACE ts_test;
DROP TABLESPACE
```

A careful design using the tablespaces, for example putting tables and indices on different devices,can improve sensibly the cluster's performance.

In 7.5 we'll take a look to the how PostgreSQL implements the tablespaces from the physical point of view.

5.8 Transactions

PostgreSQL implements the atomicity, the consistency and the isolation with the MVCC. The Multi Version Concurrency Controloffers high efficiency in the concurrent user accesss.

The MVCC logic is somewhat simple. When a transaction starts a write operation gets a transaction id, called XID, a 32 bit quantity. The XID value is used to determine the transaction's visibility, its relative position in an arbitrary timeline. All the transactions with XID smaller than the current XID in committed status are considered in the past and then visible. All the transactions with XID bigger than the current XID are in the future and therefore invisible.

The check is made at tuple level using two system fields xmin and xmax. When a new tuple is created the xmin is set with the transaction's xid. This field is also referred as the insert's transaction id. When a tuple is deleted then the xmax value is updated to the delete's xid. The xmax field is also know as the delete's transaction id. The tuple is not physically removed in order to ensure the read consistency for any transaction in the tuple's past. The tuples having the xmax not set are live tuples. Therefore the tuples which xmax is set are dead tuples. In this model there is no field dedicated to the update which is an insert insert combined with a delete. The update's transaction id is used either for the new tuple's xmin and the old tuple's xmax.

The dead tuples are removed by VACUUM when no longer required by existing transactions. For the tuple detailed description check 7.3.

Alongside with xmin and xmax there are cmin and cmax which data type is the command id, CID. Those fields store the internal transaction's commands in order to avoid the command to be executed on the same tuple multiple times. One practical effect of those fiels is to solve the database's Halloween Problem described there http://en.wikipedia.org/wiki/Halloween_Problem.

The SQL standard defines four level of the transaction's isolation. Each level allows or deny the following transaction's anomalies.

- **dirty read**, when a transaction can access the data written by a concurrent not committed transaction.

- **non repeatable read**, when a transaction repeats a previous read and finds the data changed by another transaction which has committed since the initial read.

- **phantom read**, when a transaction executes a previous query and finds a different set of rows with the same search condition because the results was changed by another committed transaction

The table 5.2 shows the transaction's isolation levels and which anomalies are possible or not within. PostgreSQL supports the minimum isolation level to read committed. Setting the isolation level to read uncommited does not cause an error. However, the system adjusts silently the level to read committed.

Isolation Level	Dirty Read	Nonrepeatable Read	Phantom Read
Read uncommitted	Possible	Possible	Possible
Read committed	Not possible	Possible	Possible
Repeatable read	Not possible	Not possible	Possible
Serializable	Not possible	Not possible	Not possible

Table 5.2: SQL Transaction isolation levels

The isolation level can be set per session with the command SET TRANSACTION ISOLATION LEVEL.

```
SET TRANSACTION ISOLATION LEVEL { SERIALIZABLE | REPEATABLE READ | READ
COMMITTED | READ UNCOMMITTED };
```

It's also possible to change the isolation level cluster wide changing the GUC parameter transaction_isolation.

5.8.1   Snapshot exports

PostgreSQL 9.2 introduced the transaction's snapshot exports. A session with an open transaction, can export its snapshot to other sessions. The snapshot can be imported as long as the exporting transaction is in progress. This feature opens some interesting scenarios where multiple backends can import a consistent snapshot and run, for example, read queries in parallel. One brilliant snapshot export's implementation is the parallel export available with the 9.3's pg_dump. Check 9.3 for more information.

An example will help us to explain better the concept. We'll use the table created in 5.6. The first thing to do is connecting to the cluster and start a new transaction with at least the REPEATABLE READ isolation level. Then the function pg_export_snapshot() is used to get the snapshot's identifier.

```
postgres=# BEGIN TRANSACTION ISOLATION LEVEL REPEATABLE READ;
BEGIN
postgres=# SELECT pg_export_snapshot();
 pg_export_snapshot
--------------------
 00001369-1
(1 row)

postgres=# SELECT count(*) FROM t_data;
 count
-------
   200
(1 row)
```

Connectin with another backend let's remove all the rows from the table t_data table.

```
postgres=# DELETE FROM t_data;
DELETE 200
postgres=# SELECT count(*) FROM t_data;
 count
-------
     0
(1 row)
```

After importing the snapshot 00001369-1 the rows are back in place.

```
postgres=# BEGIN TRANSACTION ISOLATION LEVEL REPEATABLE READ;
BEGIN
postgres=# SET TRANSACTION SNAPSHOT '00001369-1';
SET
postgres=# SELECT count(*) FROM t_data;
 count
-------
   200
(1 row)
```

It's important to use at least the REPEATABLE READ as isolation level. Using the READ COMMITTED for the export does not generates an error. However the snapshot is discarded immediately because the READ COMMITTED takes a new snapshot for each command.

Chapter 6

Data integrity

There is only one thing worse than losing the database. When the data is rubbish. In this chapter we'll have a brief look to the constraints available in PostgreSQL and how they can be used to preserve the data integrity..

A constraint, like the name suggest enforces one or more restrictions over the table's data. When the restriction enforces the data on the relation where the constraint is defined, then the constraint is local. When the constraints validates the local using the data in a different relation then the constraint is foreign.

The constraints can be defined like table or column constraint. The table constraints are defined at table level, just after the field's list. A column constraint is defined in the field's definition after the data type.

When a constraint is created the enforcement applies immediately. At creation time the table's data is validated against the constraint. If any validation error, then the creation aborts. However, the foreign keys and the check constraints can be created without the initial validation using the clause NOT VALID. This clause tells PostgreSQL to not validate the constraint's enforcement on the existing data, improving the creation's speed.

6.1 Primary keys

A primary key enforces the uniqueness of the participating fields. The uniqueness is enforced at the strictest level because even the NULL values are not permitted. The primary key creates an implicit unique index on the key's fields. Because the index creation requires the read lock this can cause downtime. In 8.3 is explained a method which in some cases helps to minimise the disruption. A table can have only one primary key.

A primary key can be defined with the table or column constraint's syntax.

```
--PRIMARY KEY AS TABLE CONSTRAINT
CREATE TABLE t_table_cons
        (
                i_id            serial,
                v_data          character varying (255),
                CONSTRAINT pk_t_table_cons PRIMARY KEY (i_id)
        )
;


--PRIMARY KEY AS COLUMN CONSTRAINT
CREATE TABLE t_column_cons
        (
                i_id            serial PRIMARY KEY,
                v_data          character varying (255)
        )
;
```

With the table constraint syntax it's possible to specify the constraint name.

The previous example shows the most common primary key implementation. The constraint is defined over a serial field. The serial type is a shortcut for **integer NOT NULL** with the default value set by an auto generated sequence. The sequence's upper limit is 9,223,372,036,854,775,807. However the integer's upper limit is just 2,147,483,647. On tables with a high generation for the key's new values the bigserial should be used instead of serial. Changing the field's type is still possible but unfortunately this requires a complete table's rewrite.

```
postgres=# SET client_min_messages='debug5';
postgres=# ALTER TABLE t_table_cons ALTER COLUMN i_id SET DATA TYPE  bigint;
DEBUG:   StartTransactionCommand
DEBUG:   StartTransaction
DEBUG:   name: unnamed; blockState:          DEFAULT; state: INPROGR, xid/subid/cid
    : 0/1/0, nestlvl: 1,
children:
DEBUG:   ProcessUtility
DEBUG:   drop auto-cascades to index pk_t_table_cons
DEBUG:   rewriting table "t_table_cons"
DEBUG:   building index "pk_t_table_cons" on table "t_table_cons"
DEBUG:   drop auto-cascades to type pg_temp_51718
DEBUG:   drop auto-cascades to type pg_temp_51718[]
DEBUG:   CommitTransactionCommand
DEBUG:   CommitTransaction
DEBUG:   name: unnamed; blockState:          STARTED; state: INPROGR, xid/subid/cid
    : 9642/1/14, nestlvl: 1,
children:
ALTER TABLE
```

The primary keys can be configured as natural keys, with the field's values meaningful in the real world. For example a table storing the cities will have the field v_city as primary key instead of the surrogate key i_city_id.

```
--PRIMARY NATURAL KEY
CREATE TABLE t_cities
        (
                v_city            character varying (255),
                CONSTRAINT pk_t_cities PRIMARY KEY (v_city)
        )
;
```

This results in a more compact table with the key values already indexed.

6.2   Unique keys

The unique keys are very similar to the primary keys. They enforce the uniqueness using an implicit index but the NULL values are permitted. Actually a primary key is the combination of a unique key and the NOT NULL constraint. The unique keys are useful when the uniqueness should be enforced on fields not participating to the primary key.

6.3   Foreign keys

A foreign key is a constraint which ensures the data is compatible with the values stored in a foreign table's field. The typical example is when two tables need to enforce a relationship. For example let's consider a table storing the addresses.

```
CREATE TABLE t_addresses
        (
                i_id_address      serial,
                v_address         character varying(255),
                v_city            character varying(255),
                CONSTRAINT pk_t_addresses PRIMARY KEY (i_id_address)
        )
;
```

Being the city a value which can be the same for many addresses is more efficient to store the city name into a separate table and set a relation to the address table.

```
CREATE TABLE t_addresses
        (
                i_id_address      serial,
                v_address         character varying(255),
                i_id_city         integer NOT NULL,
                CONSTRAINT pk_t_addresses PRIMARY KEY (i_id_address)
        )
;

CREATE TABLE t_cities
        (
                i_id_city    serial,
                v_city       character varying(255),
                CONSTRAINT pk_t_cities PRIMARY KEY (i_id_city)
        )
;
```

61

The main problem with this structure is the consistency between the tables. Without constraints there is no validation for the city identifier. Invalid values will make the table's join invalid. The same will happen if for any reason the city identifier in the table t_cities is changed.

Enforcing the relation with a foreign key will solve both of the problems.

```
ALTER TABLE t_addresses
  ADD CONSTRAINT fk_t_addr_to_t_city
  FOREIGN KEY (i_id_city)
  REFERENCES t_cities(i_id_city)
  ;
```

The foreign key works in two ways. When a row with an invalid i_id_city hits the table t_addresses the key is violated and the insert aborts. Deleting or updating a row from the table t_cities still referenced in the table t_addresses, violates the key as well.

The enforcement is performed using the triggers. When performing a data only dump/restore, the foreign keys will not allow the restore for some tables. The option –disable-trigger allows the restore on the existing schema to succeed. For more information on this topic check 9 and 10.

The many options available with the FOREIGN KEYS give us great flexibility. The referenced table can drive different actions on the referencing data using the two event options ON DELETE and ON UPDATE. The event requires an action to perform when fired. By default this is NO ACTION which checks the constraint only at the end of the transaction. This is useful with the deferred keys. The other two actions are the RESTRICT which does not allow the deferring and the CASCADE which cascades the action to the referred rows.

For example, let's create a foreign key restricting the delete without deferring and cascading the updates.

```
ALTER TABLE t_addresses
  ADD CONSTRAINT fk_t_addr_to_t_city
  FOREIGN KEY (i_id_city)
  REFERENCES t_cities(i_id_city)
  ON UPDATE CASCADE ON DELETE RESTRICT
  ;
```

Another useful clause available only with the foreign keys and check is the NOT VALID. Creating a constraint with NOT VALID tells PostgreSQL the data is already validated by the database developer. The initial check is then skipped and the constraint creation is instantaneous. The constraint is then enforced only for the new data. The invalid constraint can be validated later with the command VALIDATE CONSTRAINT.

```
postgres=#ALTER TABLE t_addresses
              ADD CONSTRAINT fk_t_addr_to_t_city
              FOREIGN KEY (i_id_city)
              REFERENCES t_cities(i_id_city)
              ON UPDATE CASCADE ON DELETE RESTRICT
              NOT VALID
```

```
                    ;
ALTER TABLE
postgres=# ALTER TABLE t_addresses VALIDATE CONSTRAINT fk_t_addr_to_t_city ;
ALTER TABLE
```

6.4   Check constraints

A check constraint is a custom check enforcing a specific condition on the table's data. The definition can be a boolean expression or a used defined function returning a boolean value. Like the foreign keys, the check accepts the NOT VALID clause.

The check is satisfied if the condition returns true or NULL. This behaviour can produce unpredictable results if not fully understood. An example will help to clarify the behaviour. Let's add a CHECK constraint on the v_address table in order to have no zero length addresses. The insert with just the city succeed without key violation though.

```
postgres=# ALTER TABLE t_addresses
               ADD CONSTRAINT chk_t_addr_city_exists
               CHECK (length(v_address)>0)
               ;
postgres=# INSERT INTO t_cities (v_city) VALUES ('Brighton') RETURNING
    i_id_city;
 i_id_city
-----------
         2

postgres=# INSERT INTO t_addresses (i_id_city) VALUES (2);
INSERT 0 1
```

This is possible because the field v_address does not have a default value which defaults to NULL when not listed in the insert. The check constraint is correctly violated if, for example we'll try to update the v_address with the empty string.

```
postgres=# UPDATE t_addresses SET v_address ='' ;
ERROR:  new row for relation "t_addresses" violates check constraint "
    chk_t_addr_city_exists"
DETAIL:  Failing row contains (3, , 2)
```

Changing the default value for the v_address field to the empty string, will make the check constraint working as expected.

```
postgres=# ALTER TABLE t_addresses ALTER COLUMN v_address SET DEFAULT '';
ALTER TABLE
postgres=# INSERT INTO t_addresses (i_id_city) VALUES (2);
ERROR:  new row for relation "t_addresses" violates check constraint "
    chk_t_addr_city_exists"
DETAIL:  Failing row contains (4, , 2).
```

Please note the existing rows are not affected by the default value change.

6.5 Not null

The NULL value is strange. When a NULL value is stored the resulting field entry is an empty object without any type or even meaning which doesn't consumes physical space. Without specifications when a new field this is defined accepts the NULL values.

When dealing with the NULL it's important to remind that the NULL acts like the mathematical zero. When evaluating an expression where an element is NULL then the entire expression becomes NULL.

As seen before the fields with NULL values are usable for the unique constraints. Otherwise the primary key does not allow the NULL values. The NOT NULL is a column constraint which does not allow the presence of NULL values.

Actually a field with the NOT NULL the unique constraint defined is exactly what the PRIMARY KEY enforces.

For example, if we want to add the NOT NULL constraint to the field v_address in the t_addresses table the command is just.

```
postgres=# ALTER TABLE t_addresses ALTER COLUMN v_address SET NOT NULL;
ERROR:  column "v_address" contains null values
```

In this case the alter fails because the column v_address contains NULL values from the example seen in 6.4. The fix is quick and easy.

```
postgres=# UPDATE t_addresses
           SET v_address='EMPTY'
           WHERE v_address IS NULL;
UPDATE 1
postgres=# ALTER TABLE t_addresses ALTER COLUMN v_address SET NOT NULL;
ALTER TABLE
```

When adding new NULLable columns is instantaneous. PostgreSQL simply adds the new attribute in the system catalogue and manages the new tuple structure considering the new field as empty space. When the NOT NULL constraint is enforced, adding a new field requires the DEFAULT value set as well. This is an operation to consider carefully when dealing with large data sets because the table will be completely rewritten. This requires an exclusive lock on the affected relation. A better way to proceed adding a NULLable field. Afterwards the new field will be set with the expected default value. Finally a table's update will fix the NULL values without exclusive locks. When everything is fine, finally, the NOT NULL could be enforced on the new field.

Chapter 7

The physical layout

After looking to the logical structure we'll now dig into PostgreSQL's physical structure. We'll start with the top layer, looking into the data area. We'll take a look first to the data files and how they are organised. Then we'll move inside them, where the data pages and the fundamental storage unit, the tuples, are stored. A section is dedicated to the TOAST tables. The chapter will end with the physical aspect of the tablespaces and the MVCC.

7.1 Data files

As seen in 4.6 the data files are stored into the $PGDATA/base directory, organised per database object identifier. This is true also for the relations created on a different tablespace. Inside the database directories there are many files which name is numeric as well. When a new relation is created, the name is set initially to the relation's object identifier. The relation's file name can change if any actiont like REINDEX or VACUUM FULL is performed on the relation.

The data files are organised in multiple segments, each one of 1 GB and numbered with a suffix. However the first segment created is without suffix. Alongside the main data files there are some additional forks needed used by PostgreSQL for tracking the data visibility and free space.

7.1.1 Free space map

The free space map is a segment present alongside the index and table's data files . It have the same the relation's name with the suffix _fsm. PostgreSQL stores the information of the free space available.

7.1.2 Visibility map

The table's data file have a visibility map file which suffix is _vm. PostgreSQL tracks the data pages with all the tuples visible to the active transactions. This fork is also used for running the index only scans.

7.1.3 Initialisation fork

The initialisation fork is an empty file used to re initialise the unlogged relations when the cluster performs a crash recovery.

7.1.4 pg_class

When connecting to a database, all the relations inside it are listed in the pg_class system table. The field relfilenode stores the relation's filename. The system field oid, which is hidden when selecting with the wildcard *, is just the relation's object identifier and should not be used for the physical mapping.

However, PostgreSQL have many useful functions which retrieve the information using the relation's OID. For example the function pg_total_relation_size(regclass) returns the disk space used by the table, including the additional forks and the eventual TOAST table, andthe indices. The function returns the size in bytes. Another function, the pg_size_pretty(bigint), returns a human readable format for better reading.

The pg_class's field relkind is used to store the relation's kind.

Value	Relation's kind
r	ordinary table
i	index
S	sequence
v	view
m	materialised view
c	composite type
t	TOAST table
f	foreign table

Table 7.1: Relkind values

7.2 Pages

Each datafile is a collection of elements called pages. The default size is for a data page is 8 kb. The page size can be changed only recompiling the sources with the different configuration and re initialising the data area. Table's pages are also known as heap pages. The index pages have almost the same heap structure except for the special space allocated in the page's bottom. The figure 7.1 shows an index page structure. The special space is used to store information needed by the relation's structure. For example a B-tree index puts in the special space the pointers to the pages below in the B-tree structure.

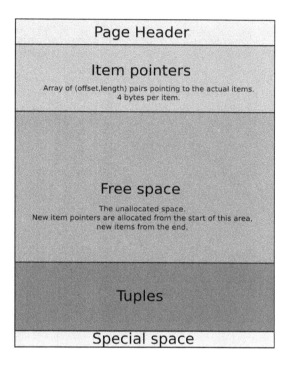

Figure 7.1: Index page

A data page starts with a header of 24 bytes. After the header there are the item pointers, which size is usually 4 bytes. Each item pointer is an array of pairs composed by the offset and the length of the item which ponints the physical tuples in the page's bottom.

The page header holds the information for the page's generic space management as shown in figure 7.2.

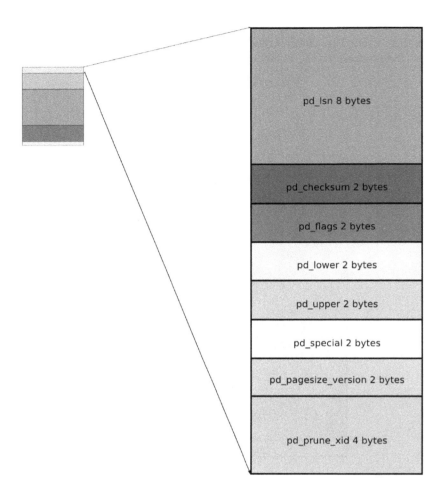

Figure 7.2: Page header

- **pd_lsn** identifies the xlog record for last page's change. The buffer manager uses the LSN for enforcing the WAL mechanism. A dirty buffer is not dumped to the disk until the xlog has been flushed at least as far as the page's LSN.

- **pd_checksum** stores the page's checksum if is enabled.

- **pd_flags** is used to store the page's various flags

- **pg_lower** is the offset to the start of the free space

- **pg_upper** is the offset to the end of the free space

- **pg_special** is the offset to the start of the special space

- **pd_pagesize_version** is the page size and the page version packed together in a single field.

- **pg_prune_xid** is a hint field to determine if the tuple's pruning is useful. Is set only on the heap pages.

The pd_checksum field replaces the pd_tli field present in the page header until PostgreSQL 9.2 which was used to track the xlog records across the timeline id.

The page's checksum is a new 9.3's feature which can detects the page corruption. It can be enabled only when the data area is initialised with initdb.

The offset fields, pg_lower, pd_upper and the optional pd_special, are 2 bytes long limiting the max page size to 32KB.

The field for the page version was introduced with PostgreSQL 7.3. Table 7.2 shows the page version number for the major versions.

PostgreSQL version	Page version
> 8.3	4
8.1,8.2	3
8.0	2
7.4,7.3	1
< 7.3	0

Table 7.2: PostgreSQL page version

7.3 Tuples

The tuples are the fundamental storage unit in PostgreSQL. They are organised as array of items which kind is initially unknown, the datum. Each tuple have a fixed header of 23 bytes as shown in the figure 7.3.

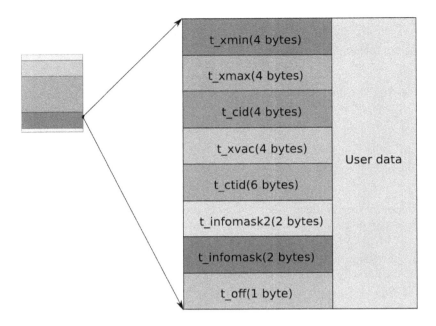

Figure 7.3: Tuple structure

The fields t_xmin and t_xmax are used to track the tuple's visibility as seen in 7.6. The field t_cid is a "virtual" field and is used either for cmin and cmax.

The field t_xvac is used by VACUUM when moving the rows, according with the source code's comments in src/include/access/htup_details.h this field is used only by the old style VACUUM FULL.

The field t_cid is the tuple's physical location identifier. Is composed by a couple of integers representing the page number and the tuple's index along the page. When a new tuple is created t_cid is set to the actual row's value. When the tuple is updated the this value changes to the new tuple's version location. This field is used in pair with t_xmax to check if the tuple is the last version. The two infomask fields are used to store various flags like the presence of the tuple's OID or if the tuple have NULL values. The last field t_off is used to set the offset to the actual tuple's data. This field's value is usually zero if the table doesn't have NULLable fields or is created WITHOUT OIDS. If the tuples have the OID and or a NULLable fields, the object identifier and a NULL bitmap are stored immediately after the tuple's header. The bitmap if present begins just after the tuple's header and consumes enough bytes to have one bit per data column. The OID if present is stored after the bitmap and consumes 4 bytes. The tuple's data is a stream of composite data described by the composite model stored in

70

the system catalogue.

7.4 TOAST

The oversize attribute storage technique is the PostgreSQL implementation for storing the data which overflows the page size. PostgreSQL does not allow the tuples spanning multiple pages. However is possible to store large amount of data which is compressed or split in multiple rows in an external TOAST table. The mechanism is completely transparent from the user's point of view.

The storage model treats the fixed length, like the integers, and the variable length types, like text, in a different way. The fixed length types which cannot produce large data are not processed through the TOAST routines. The variable length types are TOASTable if the first 32-bit word of any stored value contains the total length of the value in bytes (including itself).

The kind of the TOAST is stored in the first two bits[1] of the varlena length word. When both bits are zero then the attribute is an unTOASTed data type. In the remaining bits is stored the datum size in bytes including the length word.

If the first bit is set then the value have only a single-byte header instead of the four byte header. In the remaining bits is stored the total datum size in bytes including the length byte. This scenario have a special case uf the remaining bits are all zero. This means the value is a pointer to an out of line data stored in a separate TOAST table which structure is shown in figure 7.4.

Finally, whether is the first bit, if the second bit is set then the corresponding datum is compressed and must be decompressed before the use.

Because the TOAST usurps the first two bits of the varlena length word it limits the max stored size to 1 GB ($2^{30} - 1 bytes$) .

---

[1]On the big-endian architecture those are the high-order bits; on the little-endian those are the low-order bits

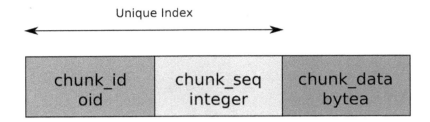

Figure 7.4: Toast table structure

The toast table is composed by three fields. The chunk_id is an OID used to store the chunk identifiers. The chunk_seq is an integer which stores the chunk orders. The chunk_data is a bytea field containing the the actual data converted in a binary string.

The chunk size is normally 2k and is controlled at compile time by the symbol TOAST_MAX_CHUNK_SIZE. The TOAST code is triggered by the value TOAST_TUPLE_THRESHOLD, also 2k by default. When the tuple's size is bigger than TOAST_TUPLE_THRESHOLD then the TOAST routines are triggered.

The TOAST_TUPLE_TARGET, default 2 kB, governs the compression's behaviour. PostgreSQL will compress the datum to achieve a final size lesser than TOAST_TUPLE_TARGET. Otherwise the out of line storage is used.
TOAST offers four different storage strategies. Each strategy can be changed per column using the ALTER TABLE SET STORAGE statement.

- PLAIN prevents either compression or out-of-line storage; It's the only storage available for fixed length data types.

- EXTENDED allows both compression and out-of-line storage. It is the default for most TOAST-able data types. Compression will be attempted first, then out-of-line storage if the row is still too big.

- EXTERNAL allows out-of-line storage but not compression.

- MAIN allows compression but not out-of-line storage. Actually the out-of-line storage is still performed as last resort.

The out of line storage have the advantage of leaving out the stored data from the row versioning; if the TOAST data is not affected by the update there will be no dead row for the TOAST data. That's possible because the varlena is a mere pointer to the chunks and a new row version will affect only the pointer leaving the TOAST data unchanged.
The TOAST table are stored like all the other relation's in the pg_class table, the associated

table can be found using a self join on the field reltoastrelid.

7.5 Tablespaces

PostgreSQL implements the tablespaces with the symbolic links. Inside the directory $PG-DATA/pg_tblspc there are the links to the physical location. Each link is named after the tablespace's OID. Therefore the tablespaces are available only on the systems with the symbolic link support.

Before the version 8.4 the tablespace symbolic link pointed directly to the referenced directory. This was a race condition when upgrading in place because the the location could clash with the upgraded cluster. From the version 9.0, the tablespace creates a sub directory directory in the tablespace location which is after the major version and the system catalogue version number.

```
postgres@tardis:~$ ls -l /var/lib/postgresql/pg_tbs/ts_test
total 0
drwx------ 2 postgres postgres 6 Jun  9 13:01 PG_9.3_201306121
```

The sub directory's name is a combination of the capital letters PG followed by the major version, truncated to the first two numbers, and the catalogue version number stored in the control file.

```
postgres@tardis:~$ export PGDATA=/var/lib/postgresql/9.3/main
postgres@tardis:~$ /usr/lib/postgresql/9.3/bin/pg_controldata
pg_control version number:          937
Catalog version number:             201306121
Database system identifier:         5992975355079285751
Database cluster state:             in production
pg_control last modified:           Mon 09 Jun 2014 13:05:14 UTC
.
.
.

WAL block size:                     8192
Bytes per WAL segment:              16777216
Maximum length of identifiers:      64
Maximum columns in an index:        32
Maximum size of a TOAST chunk:      1996
Date/time type storage:             64-bit integers
Float4 argument passing:            by value
```

```
Float8 argument passing:            by value
Data page checksum version:         0
```

PG_{MAJOR_VERSION\}_{CATALOGUE_VERSION_NUMBER}

Inside the container directory the data files are organised in the same way as in base directory. 4.6.

Moving a tablespace to another physical location it's not complicated but the cluster needs to be shut down. With the cluster stopped the container directory can be safely copied to the new location. The receiving directory must have the same permissions like the origin's. The symbolic link must be recreated to point to the new physical location. At the cluster's start the change will be automatically resolved from the symbolic link.

Until PostgreSQL 9.1 the tablespace location was stored into the field spclocation in the system table pg_tablespace. From the version 9.2 the spclocation field is removed and the tablespace's location is resolved on the fly using the function pg_tablespace_location(tablespace_oid).

This function can be used to query the system catalogue about the tablespaces. In this simple example the query returns the tablespace's location resolved from the OID.

```
postgres=#
            SELECT
                    pg_tablespace_location(oid),
                    spcname
            FROM
                    pg_tablespace
            ;

       pg_tablespace_location       |  spcname
------------------------------------+-----------
                                    | pg_default
                                    | pg_global
 /var/lib/postgresql/pg_tbs/ts_test | ts_test
(3 rows)
```

Because the function pg_tablespace_location returns the empty string for the system tablespaces, a better approach is combining the CASE construct with the function current_settings and build the absolute path for the system tablespaces.

```
postgres=# SELECT current_setting('data_directory');
       current_setting
-----------------------------
 /var/lib/postgresql/9.3/main
(1 row)

postgres=#
```

74

```
SELECT
        CASE
                WHEN
                                pg_tablespace_location(oid)=''
                        AND     spcname='pg_default'
                THEN
                        current_setting('data_directory')||'/base/'
                WHEN
                                pg_tablespace_location(oid)=''
                        AND     spcname='pg_global'
                THEN
                        current_setting('data_directory')||'/global/'
        ELSE
                pg_tablespace_location(oid)
        END
        AS      spclocation,

        spcname
FROM
        pg_tablespace;
                spclocation            |  spcname
-------------------------------------------+------------
 /var/lib/postgresql/9.3/main/base/    |  pg_default
 /var/lib/postgresql/9.3/main/global/  |  pg_global
 /var/lib/postgresql/pg_tbs/ts_test    |  ts_test
(3 rows)
```

Another useful function the pg_tablespace_databases(tablespace_oid) can help us to find the databases with the relations on a certain tablespace.

The following example uses this function again with a CASE construct for building the database having objects on a specific tablespace, in our example the ts_test created in 5.7.

```
db_test=#
SELECT
        datname,
        spcname,
        CASE
                WHEN
                                pg_tablespace_location(tbsoid)=''
                        AND     spcname='pg_default'
                THEN
                        current_setting('data_directory')||'/base/'
                WHEN
                                pg_tablespace_location(tbsoid)=''
                        AND     spcname='pg_global'
                THEN
                        current_setting('data_directory')||'/global/'
        ELSE
                pg_tablespace_location(tbsoid)
        END
        AS      spclocation
FROM
        pg_database dat,
        (
                SELECT
                        oid as tbsoid,
                        pg_tablespace_databases(oid) as datoid,
                        spcname
                FROM
                        pg_tablespace where spcname='ts_test'
        ) tbs
WHERE
        dat.oid=tbs.datoid
;
 datname | spcname |            spclocation
---------+---------+------------------------------------
 db_test | ts_test | /var/lib/postgresql/pg_tbs/ts_test
(1 row)
```

7.6   MVCC

The multiversion concurrency control is used in PostgreSQL to implement the transactional model seen in 5.8.

At logical level this is completely transparent to the user and the new row versions become visible after the commit, accordingly with the transaction isolation level.

At physical level we have for each new row version, the insert's XID stored into the t_xmin field which is used by the internal semantic to determine the row visibility.

Because the XID is a 32 bit quantity, it wraps at 4 billions. When this happens theoretically all the tuples should suddenly disappear because they switch from in the current XID's past to its future in the well known XID wraparound failure,. In the old PostgreSQL versions this was a serious problem which forced the administrators to dump/reload the entire cluster into a freshly initialised new data area every 4 billion of transactions.

In PostgreSQL 7.2 was introduced a new comparison method for the XID, the $modulo-2^{32}$ arithmetic. It was also introduced a special XID, the FrozenXID[2] assumed as always in the past. With the new comparison method, for any arbitrary XID exists 2 billion of transactions in the future and 2 billion transactions in the past.

When the age of the tuple's t_xmin becomes old the periodic VACUUM freezes the ageing tuple changing its t_xmin to the FrozenXID always in the past. In the pg_class and the pg_database tables there are two dedicated fields to track the age of the oldest XID. The value stored in those tables have little meaning if not processed through the function age() which shows the number of transactions between the current XID and the value stored in the system catalogue.

This following query returns all the databases, the corresponding datfrozenxid and the XID's age.

---

[2]The FrozenXID's value is 2. The docs of PostgreSQL 7.2 also mention the BootstrapXID which value is 1

```
postgres=#
      SELECT
                  datname,
                  age(datfrozenxid),
                  datfrozenxid
      FROM
                  pg_database;
   datname      |  age  | datfrozenxid
----------------+-------+--------------
 template1      | 4211  |          679
 template0      | 4211  |          679
 postgres       | 4211  |          679
 db_test        | 4211  |          679
```

When a tuple's age is more than 2 billions the tuple simply disappears from the cluster. Before the version 8.0 there was no alert or protection against the XID wraparound failure. Since then it was introduced a passive mechanism which emits messages in the activity log when the age of datfrozenxid is less than ten million transactions from the wraparound point.

A message like this is quite serious and should not be ignored.

```
WARNING:  database "test_db" must be vacuumed within 152405486 transactions
HINT:  To avoid a database shutdown, execute a database-wide VACUUM in
"test_db".
```

The autovacuum daemon in this case acts like a watchdog and starts vacuuming the tables with ageing tuples even if autovacuum is turned off in the cluster. There is another protection, quite radical, if for some reasons one of the database's datfrozenxid is at one million transactions from the wraparound point. In this case the cluster shuts down and refuse to start again. The only option in this case is to run the postgres process in single-user backend and execute the VACUUM on the affected relations.

The debian package's configuration is quite odd, putting the configuration files in the /etc/postgresql instead of the data area. The following example is the standalone backend's call for the debian's packaged default cluster main.

```
postgres@tardis:~/tempdata$ /usr/lib/postgresql/9.3/bin/postgres \
--single -D /var/lib/postgresql/9.3/main/base/ \
--config-file=/etc/postgresql/9.3/main/postgresql.conf

PostgreSQL stand-alone backend 9.3.5
backend>
```

The database interface in single user mode and does not have all the sophisticated features like the client psql. Anyway with a little knowledge of SQL it's possible to find the database(s) causing the shutdown and fix it.

```
backend> SELECT datname,age(datfrozenxid) FROM pg_database ORDER BY 2 DESC;
```

```
1: datname       (typeid = 19, len = 64, typmod = -1, byval = f)
2: age (typeid = 23, len = 4, typmod = -1, byval = t)
----
1: datname = "template1" (typeid = 19, len = 64, typmod = -1, byval = f)
2: age = "2146435072"  (typeid = 23, len = 4, typmod = -1, byval = t)
----
1: datname = "template0" (typeid = 19, len = 64, typmod = -1, byval = f)
2: age = "10"  (typeid = 23, len = 4, typmod = -1, byval = t)
----
1: datname = "postgres"  (typeid = 19, len = 64, typmod = -1, byval = f)
2: age = "10"  (typeid = 23, len = 4, typmod = -1, byval = t)
----
```

The age function shows how old is the last XID not yet frozen. In our example the template1 database have an age of 2146435072, one million transactions to the wraparound. We can then exit the backend with CTRL+D and restart it again in the in single user mode specifying the database name. A VACUUM will get rid of the problematic xid.

```
postgres@tardis:~/tempdata$ /usr/lib/postgresql/9.3/bin/postgres \
--single -D /var/lib/postgresql/9.3/main/base/ \
--config-file=/etc/postgresql/9.3/main/postgresql.conf \
template1

backend> SELECT current_database();
1: current_database (typeid = 19, len = 64, typmod = -1, byval = f)
----
1: current_database = "template1" (typeid = 19, len = 64, typmod = -1, byval = f)
----

backend> VACUUM FREEZE;
```

This procedure must be repeated for any database with very old XID.

Because the new rows generation at update time, this can lead to an unnecessary table and index bloat. PostgreSQL with the Heap Only Tuples (HOT) strategy can limit the unavoidable bloat caused by the updates. HOT's main goal is to keep the new row versions into the same page.

The MVCC is something to consider at design time. Ignoring the way PostgreSQL manages the physical tuples can result in data bloat and lead in general to poor performances.

Chapter 8

Maintenance

The database maintenance is something crucial for keeping the data access efficient. Building a proper maintenance plan is almost important like having a good disaster recovery plan.

As seen in 7.6 the update generates new tuple's version rather updating the affected field. The new tuple is stored in the next available free space in the same page or a different one. Frequent updates will in move the tuples across the data pages many and many times with a trail of dead tuples. Unfortunately those tuples although consuming physically space, are no longer visible for the new transactions and this results in the table bloat. The indices make things more complicated. When a new tuple's version is stored in a different page the index entry needs update to point the new page. The the index's ordered structure makes more difficult to find free space, resulting in an higher rate of new pages added to the relation and consequent bloat.

The following sections will explore the tools available for the relation's maintenance.

8.1 VACUUM

VACUUM is a PostgreSQL specific command which reclaims back the dead tuple's space. When executed without a target table, the command scans all the tables in the database. A regular VACUUM have some beneficial effects.

- Removes the dead tuples and updates the free space map.

- Updates the visibility map improving the index only scans.

- It freezes the tuples with ageing XID preventing the XID wraparound

The optional ANALYZE clause gathers the runtime statistics on processed table.

When run VACUUM clear the space used by the dead rows making space for the inserts and updates inside the data files. The data files are not shrunk except if there is a contiguous free space in the table's end. VACUUM in this case runs a truncate scan which can fail if there is a conflicting lock with the database activity. The VACUUM's truncate scan works only on the table's data files. The general approach for VACUUM is to have the minimum the impact on the cluster's activity. However, because the pages are rewritten, VACUUM can increase the I/O activity.

The index pages are scanned as well and the dead tuples are also cleared. The VACUUM performances on the indices are influenced by the maintenance_work_mem setting. If the table does not have indices VACUUM will run the cleanup reading the pages sequentially. If there is any index VACUUM will store in the maintenance work memory the tuple's references for the subsequent index cleanup. If the memory is not sufficient to fit all the tuples then VACUUM will stop the sequential read to execute the partial cleanup on the indices and free the maintenance worm mem.

The the maintenance_work_mem can impact sensibly on the VACUUM's performance on large tables. For example let's build build a simple table with 10 million rows.

```
postgres=# CREATE TABLE t_vacuum
        (
                i_id serial,
                ts_value timestamp with time zone DEFAULT clock_timestamp(),
                t_value text,
                CONSTRAINT pk_t_vacuum PRIMARY KEY  (i_id)
        )
;


CREATE TABLE


postgres=# INSERT INTO t_vacuum
        (t_value)
SELECT
        md5(i_cnt::text)
FROM
(
        SELECT
                generate_series(1,1000000) as i_cnt
) t_cnt
;
INSERT 0 1000000

CREATE INDEX idx_ts_value
        ON t_vacuum USING btree (ts_value);

CREATE INDEX
```

In order to have a static environment we'll disable the table's autovacuum. We'll also increase the session's verbosity display what's happening during the VACUUM's run.

```
postgres=# ALTER TABLE t_vacuum
        SET
                (
                        autovacuum_enabled = false,
                        toast.autovacuum_enabled = false
                )
;
ALTER TABLE
```

We are now executing a complete table rewrite running an UPDATE without the WHERE condition. This will create 10 millions of dead rows.

```
postgres=# UPDATE t_vacuum
        SET
                t_value = md5(clock_timestamp()::text)
;
UPDATE 1000000
```

Before running the VACUUM we'll change the maintenance_work_mem to a small value. We'll also enable the query timing.

```
postgres=# SET maintenance_work_mem ='2MB';
SET
SET client_min_messages='debug';
postgres=# \timing
Timing is on.

postgres=# VACUUM t_vacuum;
DEBUG:  vacuuming "public.t_vacuum"
DEBUG:  scanned index "pk_t_vacuum" to remove 349243 row versions
DETAIL:  CPU 0.04s/0.39u sec elapsed 2.02 sec.
DEBUG:  scanned index "idx_ts_value" to remove 349243 row versions
DETAIL:  CPU 0.05s/0.40u sec elapsed 1.05 sec.
DEBUG:  "t_vacuum": removed 349243 row versions in 3601 pages
DETAIL:  CPU 0.05s/0.05u sec elapsed 0.94 sec.
DEBUG:  scanned index "pk_t_vacuum" to remove 349297 row versions
DETAIL:  CPU 0.02s/0.25u sec elapsed 0.46 sec.
DEBUG:  scanned index "idx_ts_value" to remove 349297 row versions
DETAIL:  CPU 0.02s/0.25u sec elapsed 0.51 sec.
DEBUG:  "t_vacuum": removed 349297 row versions in 3601 pages
DETAIL:  CPU 0.07s/0.04u sec elapsed 1.92 sec.
DEBUG:  scanned index "pk_t_vacuum" to remove 301390 row versions
DETAIL:  CPU 0.01s/0.15u sec elapsed 0.19 sec.
DEBUG:  scanned index "idx_ts_value" to remove 301390 row versions
DETAIL:  CPU 0.01s/0.13u sec elapsed 0.15 sec.
DEBUG:  "t_vacuum": removed 301390 row versions in 3108 pages
DETAIL:  CPU 0.03s/0.03u sec elapsed 2.15 sec.
DEBUG:  index "pk_t_vacuum" now contains 1000000 row versions in 8237 pages
DETAIL:  999930 index row versions were removed.
```

```
0 index pages have been deleted, 0 are currently reusable.
CPU 0.00s/0.00u sec elapsed 0.00 sec.
DEBUG:  index "idx_ts_value" now contains 1000000 row versions in 8237 pages
DETAIL:  999930 index row versions were removed.
0 index pages have been deleted, 0 are currently reusable.
CPU 0.00s/0.00u sec elapsed 0.00 sec.
DEBUG:  "t_vacuum": found 1000000 removable, 1000000 nonremovable row versions
    in 20619 out of 20619 pages
DETAIL:  0 dead row versions cannot be removed yet.
There were 43 unused item pointers.
0 pages are entirely empty.
CPU 0.53s/2.05u sec elapsed 12.34 sec.
DEBUG:  vacuuming "pg_toast.pg_toast_51919"
DEBUG:  index "pg_toast_51919_index" now contains 0 row versions in 1 pages
DETAIL:  0 index row versions were removed.
0 index pages have been deleted, 0 are currently reusable.
CPU 0.00s/0.00u sec elapsed 0.00 sec.
DEBUG:  "pg_toast_51919": found 0 removable, 0 nonremovable row versions in 0
    out of 0 pages
DETAIL:  0 dead row versions cannot be removed yet.
There were 0 unused item pointers.
0 pages are entirely empty.
CPU 0.00s/0.00u sec elapsed 0.00 sec.
VACUUM
Time: 12377.436 ms
postgres=#
```

VACUUM stores in the maintenance_work_mem an array of TCID pointers to the removed dead tuples. This is used for the index cleanup. With a small maintenance_work_mem the array can consume the entire memory causing VACUUM to pause the table scan for a partial index cleanup. The table scan then resumes. Increasing the maintenance_work_mem to 2 GB[1] the index scan without pauses which improves the VACUUM's speed.

```
postgres=# SET maintenance_work_mem ='20MB';
SET

postgres=# VACUUM t_vacuum;
DEBUG:  vacuuming "public.t_vacuum"
DEBUG:  scanned index "pk_t_vacuum" to remove 999857 row versions
DETAIL:  CPU 0.07s/0.50u sec elapsed 1.38 sec.
DEBUG:  scanned index "idx_ts_value" to remove 999857 row versions
DETAIL:  CPU 0.10s/0.48u sec elapsed 3.41 sec.
DEBUG:  "t_vacuum": removed 999857 row versions in 10309 pages
DETAIL:  CPU 0.16s/0.12u sec elapsed 2.47 sec.
DEBUG:  index "pk_t_vacuum" now contains 1000000 row versions in 8237 pages
DETAIL:  999857 index row versions were removed.
0 index pages have been deleted, 0 are currently reusable.
CPU 0.00s/0.00u sec elapsed 0.00 sec.
DEBUG:  index "idx_ts_value" now contains 1000000 row versions in 8237 pages
DETAIL:  999857 index row versions were removed.
0 index pages have been deleted, 0 are currently reusable.
```

---

[1]In order to have the table in the same conditions the table was cleared with a VACUUM FULL and bloated with a new update.

```
CPU 0.00s/0.00u sec elapsed 0.00 sec.
DEBUG:  "t_vacuum": found 1000000 removable, 1000000 nonremovable row versions
    in 20619 out of 20619 pages
DETAIL:  0 dead row versions cannot be removed yet.
There were 100 unused item pointers.
0 pages are entirely empty.
CPU 0.56s/1.39u sec elapsed 9.61 sec.
DEBUG:  vacuuming "pg_toast.pg_toast_51919"
DEBUG:  index "pg_toast_51919_index" now contains 0 row versions in 1 pages
DETAIL:  0 index row versions were removed.
0 index pages have been deleted, 0 are currently reusable.
CPU 0.00s/0.00u sec elapsed 0.00 sec.
DEBUG:  "pg_toast_51919": found 0 removable, 0 nonremovable row versions in 0
    out of 0 pages
DETAIL:  0 dead row versions cannot be removed yet.
There were 0 unused item pointers.
0 pages are entirely empty.
CPU 0.00s/0.00u sec elapsed 0.00 sec.
VACUUM
Time: 9646.112 ms
```

Without the indices VACUUM completes in the shortest time.

```
postgres=# SET maintenance_work_mem ='20MB';
SET
postgres=# \timing
Timing is on.

postgres=# DROP INDEX idx_ts_value ;
DROP INDEX
Time: 59.490 ms


postgres=# ALTER TABLE t_vacuum DROP CONSTRAINT pk_t_vacuum;
DEBUG:  drop auto-cascades to index pk_t_vacuum
ALTER TABLE
Time: 182.737 ms

postgres=# VACUUM t_vacuum;
DEBUG:  vacuuming "public.t_vacuum"
DEBUG:  "t_vacuum": removed 1000000 row versions in 10310 pages
DEBUG:  "t_vacuum": found 1000000 removable, 1000000 nonremovable row versions
    in 20619 out of 20619 pages
DETAIL:  0 dead row versions cannot be removed yet.
There were 143 unused item pointers.
0 pages are entirely empty.
CPU 0.06s/0.30u sec elapsed 1.55 sec.
DEBUG:  vacuuming "pg_toast.pg_toast_51919"
DEBUG:  index "pg_toast_51919_index" now contains 0 row versions in 1 pages
DETAIL:  0 index row versions were removed.
0 index pages have been deleted, 0 are currently reusable.
CPU 0.00s/0.00u sec elapsed 0.00 sec.
DEBUG:  "pg_toast_51919": found 0 removable, 0 nonremovable row versions in 0
    out of 0 pages
```

```
DETAIL:  0 dead row versions cannot be removed yet.
There were 0 unused item pointers.
0 pages are entirely empty.
CPU 0.00s/0.00u sec elapsed 0.00 sec.
VACUUM
Time: 1581.384 ms
```

Before proceeding let's put back the primary key and the index on the relation. We'll need it later.

```
postgres=# ALTER TABLE t_vacuum ADD CONSTRAINT pk_t_vacuum PRIMARY KEY (i_id);
DEBUG:  ALTER TABLE / ADD PRIMARY KEY will create implicit index "pk_t_vacuum"
    for table "t_vacuum"
DEBUG:  building index "pk_t_vacuum" on table "t_vacuum"
ALTER TABLE
Time: 1357.689 ms

postgres=# CREATE INDEX idx_ts_value
postgres-#         ON t_vacuum USING btree (ts_value);
DEBUG:  building index "idx_ts_value" on table "t_vacuum"
CREATE INDEX
Time: 1305.911 ms
```

The table seen in the example begins with a size of 806 MB . After the update the table's size is doubled. After the VACUUM run the table does not shrink. This is caused because there is no contiguous free space in the end. The new row versions generated by the update are stored in the table's end. A second UPDATE with a new VACUUM could truncate the table if all the dead rows are in the table's end. However VACUUM's main goal is to keep the table's size stable, rather shrinking down the space.

The prevention of the XID wraparound failure managed automatically by VACUUM. When a live tuple have the t_xmin's older than the parameter vacuum_freeze_min_age, then the t_xid replaced with the FrozenXID setting the tuple safely in the past. Because VACUUM by default skips the pages without dead tuples some ageing tuples could be skipped by the run. The parameter vacuum_freeze_table_age avoids this scenario triggering a full table's VACUUM when table's relfrozenxid age exceeds the value.

It's also possible to run VACUUM with the FREEZE clause. In this case VACUUM will freeze all the tuples regardless of their age. The command is equivalent of running VACUUM with vacuum_freeze_min_age set to zero.

VACUUM is controlled by some GUC parameters.

8.1.1   vacuum_freeze_table_age

This parameter is used to start a full table VACUUM when the table's relfrozenxid exceeds the parameter's value. The default setting is 150 million of transactions. Despite the possible values are between zero and one billion, VACUUM will silently set the effective value to the

95% of the autovacuum_freeze_max_age, reducing the possibility to have an anti-wraparound autovacuum.

8.1.2   vacuum_freeze_min_age

The parameter sets minimum age for the tuple's t_xmin to be frozen. The default is 50 million transactions. The values accepted are between zero to one billion. However VACUUM will change silently the effective value to one half of autovacuum_freeze_max_age in order to maximise the time between the forced autovacuum.

8.1.3   vacuum_multixact_freeze_table_age

From PostgreSQL 9.3 VACUUM maintains the multixact ID as well. This identifier is used to store the row locks in the tuple's header. Because the multixact ID is a 32 bit quantity there is the same XID's issue with the wraparound failure. This parameter sets the value after that a table scan is performed. The setting is checked against the field relminmxid of the pg_class. The default is 150 million of multixacts. The accepted values are between zero and one billion. VACUUM limits the effective value to the 95% of autovacuum_multixact_freeze_max_age. This wat the manual VACUUM has a chance to run before an anti-wraparound autovacuum.

8.1.4   vacuum_multixact_freeze_min_age

Sets the minimum age in multixacts for VACUUM to replace the multixact IDs with a newer transaction ID or multixact ID, while scanning a table. The default is 5 million multixacts. The accepted values are between zero and one billion. VACUUM will silently limit the effective value to one half of autovacuum_multixact_freeze_max_age, in order to increase the time between the forced autovacuums.

8.1.5   vacuum_defer_cleanup_age

This parameter have effect only on the master in the hot standby configurations. When set to a positive value on the master, can reduce the risk of query conflicts on the standby. Does not have effect on a standby server.

8.1.6   vacuum_cost_delay

This parameter, if set to a not zero value enables the cost based vacuum delay and sets the sleep time, in milliseconds, for VACUUM process when the cost limit exceeds. The default value is zero, which disables the cost-based vacuum delay feature.

8.1.7   vacuum_cost_limit

This parameter sets the arbitrary cost limit. VACUUM sleeps for the time set in vacuum_cost_delay when the value is reached. The default value is 200.

8.1.8 vacuum_cost_page_hit

The parameter sets the arbitrary cost for vacuuming one buffer found in the shared buffer cache. It represents the cost to lock the buffer, look up to the shared hash table and scan the content of the page. The default value is one.

8.1.9 vacuum_cost_page_miss

This parameter sets the arbitrary cost for vacuuming a buffer not present in the shared buffer. This represents the effort to lock the buffer pool, lookup the shared hash table, read the desired block from the disk and scan its content. The default value is 10.

8.1.10 vacuum_cost_page_dirty

This parameter sets the arbitrary cost charged when vacuum scans a previously dirty page[2]. It represents the extra I/O required to flush the dirty block out to disk. The default value is 20.

8.2 ANALYZE

The PostgreSQL's query optimiser builds the query execution plan using the cost estimates from the internal runtime statistics. Each step in the execution plan gets an arbitrary cost used to compute the plan total cost. The execution plan which estimated cost is lesser is then sent to the query executor. Keeping the runtime statistics up to date helps the cluster to build efficient plans.

The command ANALYZE gathers the relation's runtime statistics. When executed reads the data, builds up the statistics and stores them into the pg_statistics system table. The command accepts the optional clause VERBOSE to increase verbosity alongside the optional target table and the eventual column list. If ANALYZE is launched with no parameters scans all the tables in the database. Specifying the table name will cause ANALYZE to process all the table's columns.

When working on large tables ANALYZE runs a sample read on the table. The GUC parameter default_statistics_target determines the amount of entries read by the sample. The default limit is 100. Increasing the value will cause the planner to get better estimates, in particular for the columns with the data distributed irregularly. This accuracy have a cost. Will cause ANALYZE to spend a longer time for the statistics gathering and building plus an bigger space required in pg_statistics.

The following example will show how default_statistics_target can affects the estimates. We'll re use the table created in 8.1. This is the result of ANALYZE VERBOSE with the default statistic target.

---

[2]A page is dirty when its modifications are not yet written on the relation's data file

```
postgres=# SET default_statistics_target =100;
SET
postgres=# ANALYZE VERBOSE t_vacuum;
INFO:   analyzing "public.t_vacuum"
INFO:   "t_vacuum": scanned 30000 of 103093 pages, containing 2909979 live rows
    and 0 dead rows;
30000 rows in sample, 9999985 estimated total rows
ANALYZE
```

The table have 10 million rows but ANALYZE estimates the contents in just 2,909,979 rows, the 30% of the effective live tuples.

Now we'll run ANALYZE with default_statistics_target set to its maximum allowed value, 10000.

```
SET
postgres=# ANALYZE VERBOSE t_vacuum;
INFO:   analyzing "public.t_vacuum"
INFO:   "t_vacuum": scanned 103093 of 103093 pages, containing 10000000 live
    rows and 0 dead rows;
3000000 rows in sample, 10000000 estimated total rows
ANALYZE
```

This time the table's live tuples are estimated correctly in 10 millions.

The table pg_statistics is not intended for human reading. The statistics are translated in human readable format by the view pg_stats.

The rule of thumb when dealing with poorly performing queries, is to check if statistics are recent and accurate. The information is stored into the view pg_stat_all_tables [3].

For example this query gets, for a certain table, the last execution of the manual and the auto vacuum alongside with the last analyze and auto analyze.

```
postgres=# \x
Expanded display is on.
postgres=# SELECT
        schemaname,
        relname,
        last_vacuum,
        last_autovacuum,
        last_analyze,
        last_autoanalyze
FROM
        pg_stat_all_tables
WHERE
        relname='t_vacuum'
;
-[ RECORD 1 ]----+------------------------------
schemaname       | public
```

---

[3]The subset views pg_stat_user_tables and pg_stat_sys_tables are useful to search respectively the current user and the system tables only.

```
relname           | t_vacuum
last_vacuum       |
last_autovacuum   |
last_analyze      | 2014-06-17 18:48:56.359709+00
last_autoanalyze  |

postgres=#
```

The statistics target is a per column setting allowing a fine grained tuning for the ANA-LYZE command.

```
--SET THE STATISTICS TO 1000 ON THE COLUMN i_id
ALTER TABLE t_vacuum
      ALTER COLUMN  i_id
                    SET STATISTICS 1000
;
```

The default statistic target can be changed for the current session only using the SET command. The cluster wide value is changed using the parameter in the postgresql.conf file.

8.3   REINDEX

The general purpose B-tree index stores the indexed value alongside with the pointer to the tuple's heap page. The index pages are organised in the form of a balanced tree linking each other using page's special space seen in 7.1. As long as the heap tuple remains in the same page the index entry doesn't need update. The HOT strategy tries to achieve this goal keeping the heap tuples in the same page. When a new tuple version is stored in the heap page then also the index entry needs to reflect the change. By default the index pages have a percentage of space reserved for the updates. This is an hardcoded 30% for the not leaf pages and a 10% for the leaf pages. The latter can be changed adjusting the index's fillfactor.

VACUUM efficiency is worse with the indices because their ordered nature. Even converting the dead tuples to free space, this is reusable only if the new entry is compatible with the B-tree position. The empty pages can be recycled but this requires at least two VACUUM runs. When an index page is empty then is marked as deleted by VACUUM but not immediately recycled. The page is first stamped with the next XID and therefore becomes invisible. Only a second VACUUM will clear the deleted pages returning the free space to the relation. This behaviour is made on purpose, because there might be running scans which still need to access the page. The second VACUUM is the safest way to recycle the page only if no longer required.

Therefore the indices are affected by the data bloat more than the tables. Alongside with a bigger disk space allocation, the bloat results generally in bad index's performances. The periodical reindex is the best way to keep the indices in good shape.

Unlike the VACUUM, the REINDEX have a noticeable impact on the cluster's activity. To ensure the data is consistently read the REINDEX sets a lock on the table preventing the table's writes. The reads are also blocked for the queries which are using the index.

A B-tree index build requires a the data to be sorted. PostgreSQL comes with a handy GUC parameter to track the sort, the trace_sort which requires a verbosity set to DEBUG.

The following example is the output of the primary key's reindex of the test table created in 8.1.

```
postgres=# SET trace_sort =on;
SET
postgres=# SET client_min_messages ='debug';
SET
postgres=# \timing
Timing is on.

postgres=# REINDEX INDEX pk_t_vacuum ;
DEBUG:  building index "pk_t_vacuum" on table "t_vacuum"
LOG:  begin index sort: unique = t, workMem = 16384, randomAccess = f
LOG:  begin index sort: unique = f, workMem = 1024, randomAccess = f
LOG:  switching to external sort with 59 tapes: CPU 0.00s/0.08u sec elapsed
   0.08 sec
LOG:  finished writing run 1 to tape 0: CPU 0.13s/3.41u sec elapsed 3.55 sec
LOG:  internal sort ended, 25 KB used: CPU 0.39s/8.35u sec elapsed 8.74 sec
LOG:  performsort starting: CPU 0.39s/8.35u sec elapsed 8.74 sec
LOG:  finished writing final run 2 to tape 1: CPU 0.39s/8.50u sec elapsed 8.89
   sec
LOG:  performsort done (except 2-way final merge): CPU 0.40s/8.51u sec elapsed
   8.90 sec
LOG:  external sort ended, 24438 disk blocks used: CPU 0.70s/9.67u sec elapsed
   11.81 sec
REINDEX
Time: 11876.807 ms
```

The reindex performs a data sort but maintenance_work_mem does not fit the table's data. PostgreSQL then starts a disk sort in order to build up the index. The way PostgreSQL determines whether sort on disk or in memory should use follow this simple rule. If after the table scan the maintenance work memory is exhausted then will be used a sort on disk. That's the reason why increasing the maintenance_work_mem can improve the reindex. Determining the correct value for this parameter is quite tricky.

This is the reindex using 1 GB for the maintenance_work_mem.

```
postgres=# \timing
Timing is on.
postgres=# SET maintenance_work_mem='1GB';
SET
Time: 0.193 ms
postgres=# REINDEX INDEX pk_t_vacuum ;
DEBUG:  building index "pk_t_vacuum" on table "t_vacuum"
LOG:  begin index sort: unique = t, workMem = 1048576, randomAccess = f
LOG:  begin index sort: unique = f, workMem = 1024, randomAccess = f
LOG:  internal sort ended, 25 KB used: CPU 0.45s/2.02u sec elapsed 2.47 sec
LOG:  performsort starting: CPU 0.45s/2.02u sec elapsed 2.47 sec
```

```
LOG:   performsort done: CPU 0.45s/4.36u sec elapsed 4.81 sec
LOG:   internal sort ended, 705717 KB used: CPU 0.66s/4.74u sec elapsed 6.85 sec
REINDEX
Time: 6964.196 ms
```

After the sort the reindex creates a new index file from the sorted data which is changed in the system catalogue's pg_class.relfilenode. When the reindex's transaction commits the old file node is deleted. The sequence can be emulated creating a new index with a different name. The old index can be dropped safely and the new one renamed to the old's name. This approach have the advantage of not blocking the table's reads using the old index.

```
postgres=# CREATE INDEX idx_ts_value_new
              ON t_vacuum USING btree (ts_value);
CREATE INDEX

postgres=# DROP INDEX idx_ts_value;
DROP INDEX
postgres=# ALTER INDEX idx_ts_value_new
              RENAME TO idx_ts_value;
ALTER INDEX
```

From the version 8.2 PostgreSQL supports the CREATE INDEX CONCURRENTLY statement which doesn't block the cluster's activity. With this method the index creation adds a new invalid index in the system catalogue then starts a table scan to build the dirty index. A second table scan is then executed to fix the invalid index entries and, after a final validation the index becomes valid.

The concurrent index build have indeed some caveats and limitations.

- Any problem with the table scan will fail the command and leaving an invalid index in place. This relation is not used for the reads but adds an extra overhead to the inserts and updates.

- When building an unique index concurrently this start enforcing the uniqueness when the second table scan starts. Some transactions could then start reporting the uniqueness violation before the index becoming available. In the case the build fails on the second table scan the invalid index will enforce the uniqueness regardless of its status.

- Regular index builds can run in parallel on the same table. Concurrent index builds cannot.

- Concurrent index builds cannot run within a transaction block.

The primary keys and unique constraints can be swapped like the indices using a different approach. PostgreSQL since the version 9.1 supports the *ALTER TABLE table_name ADD table_constraint using_index* statement. Combining a DROP CONSTRAINT with this command is possible to swap the constraint's index without losing the uniqueness enforcement.

```
postgres=# CREATE UNIQUE INDEX pk_t_vacuum_new
                ON  t_vacuum USING BTREE (i_id);
CREATE INDEX
postgres=# ALTER TABLE t_vacuum
                DROP CONSTRAINT pk_t_vacuum ,
                ADD CONSTRAINT pk_t_vacuum_new PRIMARY KEY
                        USING INDEX pk_t_vacuum_new
            ;
ALTER TABLE
postgres=# ALTER INDEX pk_t_vacuum_new
                RENAME TO pk_t_vacuum;
ALTER INDEX
```

The example uses a regular index build and then blocks the writes. It's also possible to build the new index concurrently.

This method cannot be used though if any foreign key references the local key.

```
postgres=# CREATE TABLE t_vac_foreign
                                    (
                                        i_foreign serial ,
                                        i_id integer NOT NULL ,
                                        t_value text
                                    )
            ;
CREATE TABLE
postgres=# ALTER TABLE t_vac_foreign
                ADD CONSTRAINT fk_t_vac_foreign_t_vacuum_i_id
                    FOREIGN KEY (i_id)
                    REFERENCES t_vacuum (i_id)
                    ON DELETE CASCADE
                    ON UPDATE RESTRICT;
ALTER TABLE

postgres=# CREATE UNIQUE INDEX pk_t_vacuum_new ON  t_vacuum USING BTREE (i_id);
CREATE INDEX
postgres=# ALTER TABLE t_vacuum
postgres-# DROP CONSTRAINT pk_t_vacuum ,
postgres-# ADD CONSTRAINT pk_t_vacuum_new PRIMARY KEY  USING INDEX
    pk_t_vacuum_new;
ERROR:  cannot drop constraint pk_t_vacuum on table t_vacuum because other
    objects depend on it
DETAIL:  constraint fk_t_vac_foreign_t_vacuum_i_id on table t_vac_foreign
    depends on index
pk_t_vacuum
HINT:  Use DROP ... CASCADE to drop the dependent objects too.
```

In this case the safest way to proceed is to run a conventional REINDEX.

8.4 VACUUM FULL and CLUSTER

PostgreSQL ships with two commands used to shrink the data files.

The command CLUSTER can be quite confusing. It's purpose is to rebuild a completely new table with the tuples with same order of the clustered index which is set using the command *ALTER TABLE table_name CLUSTER ON index_name*.

For example, this is the verbose output of the cluster command for the table created in 8.1. The table has been clustered on the timestamp field's index.

```
postgres=# SET trace_sort='on';
SET
postgres=# SET client_min_messages ='debug';
SET
postgres=# ALTER TABLE t_vacuum CLUSTER ON idx_ts_value ;
ALTER TABLE
postgres=# CLUSTER t_vacuum;
DEBUG:  building index "pg_toast_51949_index" on table "pg_toast_51949"
LOG:  begin index sort: unique = t, workMem = 16384, randomAccess = f
LOG:  begin index sort: unique = f, workMem = 1024, randomAccess = f
LOG:  internal sort ended, 25 KB used: CPU 0.00s/0.00u sec elapsed 0.00 sec
LOG:  performsort starting: CPU 0.00s/0.00u sec elapsed 0.00 sec
LOG:  performsort done: CPU 0.00s/0.00u sec elapsed 0.00 sec
LOG:  internal sort ended, 25 KB used: CPU 0.00s/0.00u sec elapsed 0.06 sec
LOG:  begin tuple sort: nkeys = 1, workMem = 16384, randomAccess = f
DEBUG:  clustering "public.t_vacuum" using sequential scan and sort
LOG:  switching to external sort with 59 tapes: CPU 0.02s/0.02u sec elapsed
    0.05 sec
LOG:  performsort starting: CPU 0.10s/0.71u sec elapsed 0.81 sec
LOG:  finished writing run 1 to tape 0: CPU 0.11s/0.75u sec elapsed 0.86 sec
LOG:  finished writing final run 2 to tape 1: CPU 0.11s/0.75u sec elapsed 0.86
    sec
LOG:  performsort done (except 2-way final merge): CPU 0.11s/0.76u sec elapsed
    0.87 sec
LOG:  external sort ended, 10141 disk blocks used: CPU 0.22s/1.01u sec elapsed
    1.23 sec
DEBUG:  "t_vacuum": found 0 removable, 1000000 nonremovable row versions in
    20619 pages
DETAIL:  0 dead row versions cannot be removed yet.
CPU 0.24s/1.02u sec elapsed 1.84 sec.
DEBUG:  building index "pk_t_vacuum" on table "t_vacuum"
LOG:  begin index sort: unique = f, workMem = 16384, randomAccess = f
LOG:  switching to external sort with 59 tapes: CPU 0.01s/0.07u sec elapsed
    0.09 sec
LOG:  performsort starting: CPU 0.04s/0.74u sec elapsed 0.78 sec
LOG:  finished writing final run 1 to tape 0: CPU 0.04s/0.88u sec elapsed 0.92
    sec
LOG:  performsort done: CPU 0.04s/0.88u sec elapsed 0.92 sec
LOG:  external sort ended, 2445 disk blocks used: CPU 0.07s/0.96u sec elapsed
    1.23 sec
DEBUG:  building index "idx_ts_value" on table "t_vacuum"
LOG:  begin index sort: unique = f, workMem = 16384, randomAccess = f
LOG:  switching to external sort with 59 tapes: CPU 0.00s/0.07u sec elapsed
    0.08 sec
LOG:  performsort starting: CPU 0.02s/0.74u sec elapsed 0.76 sec
LOG:  finished writing final run 1 to tape 0: CPU 0.02s/0.88u sec elapsed 0.91
    sec
```

```
LOG:   performsort done: CPU 0.02s/0.88u sec elapsed 0.91 sec
LOG:   external sort ended, 2445 disk blocks used: CPU 0.04s/0.98u sec elapsed
    1.21 sec
DEBUG:   drop auto-cascades to type pg_temp_51919
DEBUG:   drop auto-cascades to type pg_temp_51919[]
DEBUG:   drop auto-cascades to toast table pg_toast.pg_toast_51949
DEBUG:   drop auto-cascades to index pg_toast.pg_toast_51949_index
DEBUG:   drop auto-cascades to type pg_toast.pg_toast_51949
CLUSTER
postgres=#
```

CLUSTER have different strategies to order the data. In this example the chosen strategy is the sequential scan and sort strategy. The tuples are stored into a new file node which is assigned to the relation's relfilenode. Before completing the operation the indices are reindexed. When the CLUSTER is done the old file node is removed from the disk. The process is quite invasive though. Because the relation is literally rebuilt from scratch it requires an exclusive access lock which blocks the reads and the writes. The storage is another critical point. There should be enough to keep old relation's data files, with the new files plus the indices and the eventual sort on disk.

Taking a look to source code in **src/backend/commands/cluster.c**, show us how CLUSTER and VACUUM FULL do the same job with a slight difference. VACUUM FULL does not sort the new relation's data..

VACUUM FULL and CLUSTER have some beneficial effects on the disk storage as the space is returned to the operating system and improve the indices performance because the implicit reindex.

The blocking nature of those commands have an unavoidable impact on the cluster's activity. Unlike the conventional VACUUM, CLUSTER and VACUUM FULL should run when the cluster is not in use or in a maintenance window. CLUSTER and VACUUM FULL do not fix the XID wraparound failure.

As rule of thumb, in order to minimise the database's downtime, CLUSTER and VACUUM FULL should be used only for the extraordinary maintenance and only if the disk space is critical.

8.5   The autovacuum

The autovacuum daemon was introduced in the revolutionary PostgreSQL 8.0. From the version 8.3 was enabled by default because reliable and efficient. With autovacuum turned on the maintenance and the statistic gathering is done automatically by the cluster. Turning off autovacuum it doesn't disable completely the daemon. Actually the workers are started automatically to prevent the XID and multixact ID wraparound failure, regardless of the setting. In order to have autovacuum working the statistic collector must be enabled with track_counts= 'on'.

The following parameters control the autovacuum behaviour.

8.5.1   autovacuum

This parameter is used to enable or disable the autovacuum daemon. Changing the setting requires the cluster's restart.

8.5.2   autovacuum_max_workers

The parameter sets the maximum number of autovacuum subprocesses. Changing the setting requires the cluster's restart. Each subprocess consumes one PostgreSQL connection.

8.5.3   autovacuum_naptime

The parameter sets the delay between two autovacuum runs on a specified database.The delay is measured in seconds and the default value is 1 minute.

8.5.4   autovacuum_vacuum_scale_factor

The parameter one specifies the fraction of the relation's live tuples to add to the set in value in autovacuum_vacuum_threshold in order to determine whether start the automatic VACUUM. The default is 0.2, which is the table's 20%. This setting can be overridden for individual tables by changing the storage parameters.

8.5.5   autovacuum_vacuum_threshold

This parameter sets the extra threshold of updated or deleted tuples to add to the value determined from autovacuum_vacuum_scale_factor. The value is used to trigger an automatic VACUUM. The default is 50 tuples. This setting can be overridden for individual tables by changing the storage parameters. For example a table with 10 million rows and autovacuum_vacuum_threshold, autovacuum_vacuum_scale_factor set both to their default values, the autovacuum will start after when 2,000,050 tuples are updated or deleted.

8.5.6   autovacuum_analyze_scale_factor

The parameter specifies the fraction of table to add to autovacuum_analyze_threshold in order to determine whether start the automatic ANALYZE. The default is 0.1, which is the table's 10%. This setting can be overridden for individual tables by changing storage parameters.

8.5.7   autovacuum_analyze_threshold

This parameter sets the extra threshold of updated or deleted tuples to add to the value determined from autovacuum_analyze_scale_factor. The value is used to trigger an automatic ANALYZE. The default is 50 tuples. This setting can be overridden for individual tables by changing the storage parameters. For example a table with 10 million rows and autovacuum_analyze_scale_factor, autovacuum_analyze_threshold set both to their default values will start an automatic ANALYZE when 1,000,050 tuples are updated or deleted.

8.5.8   autovacuum_freeze_max_age

The parameter sets the maximum age for the pg_class's relfrozenxid. When the value is exceeded then an automatic VACUUM is forced on the relation to prevent the XID wraparound. The process will start even if the autovacuum is turned off. The parameter can be set only at server's start but is possible to set the value per table by changing the storage parameters.

8.5.9   autovacuum_multixact_freeze_max_age

The parameter sets the maximum age of the table's pg_class's relminmxid. When the value is exceeded then an automatic VACUUM is forced on the relation to prevent the multixact ID wraparound. The process will start even if the autovacuum is turned off. The parameter can be set only at server's start but is possible to set the value per table by changing the storage parameters.

8.5.10   autovacuum_vacuum_cost_delay

The parameter sets the cost delay to use in the automatic VACUUM operations. If set to -1, the regular vacuum_cost_delay value will be used. The default value is 20 milliseconds.

8.5.11   autovacuum_vacuum_cost_limit

The parameter sets cost limit value to be used in the automatic VACUUM operations. If set to -1 then the regular vacuum_cost_limit value will be used. The default value is -1. The value is distributed among the running autovacuum workers. The sum of the limits of each worker never exceeds this variable. More information on cost based vacuum here 8.1.6.

Chapter 9

Backup

The hardware is subject to faults. In particular if the storage is lost the entire data infrastructure becomes inaccessible, sometime for good. Also human errors, like wrong delete or table drop can happen. A solid backup strategy is the best protection against these problems and much more. The chapter covers the logical backup with pg_dump.

9.1 pg_dump at glance

As seen in 3.1.5, pg_dump is the PostgreSQL's utility for saving consistent snapshots of the databases. The usage is quite simple and if launched without options it tries to connect to the local cluster with the current user redirecting the dump's output to the standard output.

The help gives many useful information.

```
postgres@tardis:~/dump pg_dump --help
pg_dump dumps a database as a text file or to other formats.

Usage:
  pg_dump [OPTION]... [DBNAME]

General options:
  -f, --file=FILENAME          output file or directory name
  -F, --format=c|d|t|p         output file format (custom, directory, tar,
                               plain text (default))
  -j, --jobs=NUM               use this many parallel jobs to dump
  -v, --verbose                verbose mode
  -V, --version                output version information, then exit
  -Z, --compress=0-9           compression level for compressed formats
  --lock-wait-timeout=TIMEOUT  fail after waiting TIMEOUT for a table lock
  -?, --help                   show this help, then exit
```

```
Options controlling the output content:
  -a, --data-only              dump only the data, not the schema
  -b, --blobs                  include large objects in dump
  -c, --clean                  clean (drop) database objects before recreating
  -C, --create                 include commands to create database in dump
  -E, --encoding=ENCODING      dump the data in encoding ENCODING
  -n, --schema=SCHEMA          dump the named schema(s) only
  -N, --exclude-schema=SCHEMA  do NOT dump the named schema(s)
  -o, --oids                   include OIDs in dump
  -O, --no-owner               skip restoration of object ownership in
                               plain-text format
  -s, --schema-only            dump only the schema, no data
  -S, --superuser=NAME         superuser user name to use in plain-text format
  -t, --table=TABLE            dump the named table(s) only
  -T, --exclude-table=TABLE    do NOT dump the named table(s)
  -x, --no-privileges          do not dump privileges (grant/revoke)
  --binary-upgrade             for use by upgrade utilities only
  --column-inserts             dump data as INSERT commands with column names
  --disable-dollar-quoting     disable dollar quoting, use SQL standard quoting
  --disable-triggers           disable triggers during data-only restore
  --exclude-table-data=TABLE   do NOT dump data for the named table(s)
  --inserts                    dump data as INSERT commands, rather than COPY
  --no-security-labels         do not dump security label assignments
  --no-synchronized-snapshots  do not use synchronized snapshots in parallel jobs
  --no-tablespaces             do not dump tablespace assignments
  --no-unlogged-table-data     do not dump unlogged table data
  --quote-all-identifiers      quote all identifiers, even if not key words
  --section=SECTION            dump named section (pre-data, data, or post-data)
  --serializable-deferrable    wait until the dump can run without anomalies
  --use-set-session-authorization
                               use SET SESSION AUTHORIZATION commands instead of
                               ALTER OWNER commands to set ownership

Connection options:
  -d, --dbname=DBNAME          database to dump
  -h, --host=HOSTNAME          database server host or socket directory
  -p, --port=PORT              database server port number
  -U, --username=NAME          connect as specified database user
  -w, --no-password            never prompt for password
  -W, --password               force password prompt (should happen automatically)
  --role=ROLENAME              do SET ROLE before dump
```

9.1.1 Connection options

The connection options are used to specify the way the program connects to the cluster. All the options are straightforward except for the password. Usually the PostgreSQL clients don't accept the plain password as parameter. However is still possible to connect without specifying the password using the environmental variable PGPASSWORD or using the password file.

Using the variable PGPASSWORD is considered not secure and shouldn't be used if not trusted users are accessing the server. The password file is a text file named saved in the users's home directory as .pgpass . The file must be readable only by the user, otherwise the client will refuse to read it.
Each line specifies a connection in a fixed format.

```
hostname:port:database:username:password
```

The following example specifies the password for the connection to the host tardis, port 5432, database db_test and user usr_test.

```
tardis:5432:db_test:usr_test:testpwd
```

9.1.2 General options

The general options are used to control the backup's output and format.
The switch -f sends the backup on the specified FILENAME.

The switch -F specifies the backup format and requires a second option to tell pg_dump which format to use. The allowed formats are *c d t p* respectively *custom directory tar plain*.

If the parameter is omitted pg_dump uses the plain text format. not compressed and suitable for the direct load using psql.

The the custom and the directory format are the most versatile backup formats. They give compression and flexibility at restore time. Both have the parallel and selective restore option.

The directory format stores the schema dump in a toc file. Each table's content is then saved in a compressed file inside the target directory specified with the -f switch. From the version 9.3 this format allows the parallel dump functionality.

The tar format stores the dump in the well known tape archive format. This format is compatible with the directory format, does not compress the data and there is the limit of 8 GB for the individual table.

The -j option specifies the number of jobs to run in parallel when dumping the data. This feature is available from the version 9.3 and uses the transaction's snapshot export to have a consistent dump over the multiple export jobs. The switch is usable only with the directory format and only with PostgreSQL 9.2 and later.

The option -Z specifies the compression level for the compressed formats. The default is 5 resulting in a dumped archive from 5 to 8 times smaller than the original database.

The option –lock-wait-timeout is the number of milliseconds for the table's lock acquisition. When expired the dump will fail. Is useful to avoid the program to wait forever for a table lock but can result in failed backups if value is too much low.

9.1.3 Output options

The output options control backup output. Some of those options are meaningful only under certain conditions, some others are quite obvious.

The -a option sets the data only export. Separating schema and data have some effects at restore time, in particular with the performance. We'll see in the detail in 10 how to build an efficient two phase restore.

The -b option exports the large objects. This is the default setting except if the -n switch is used. In this case the -b is required to export the large objects.

The options -c and -C are meaningful only for the plain output format. They respectively add the DROP and CREATE command before the object's DDL. For the archive formats the same option exists for pg_restore.

The -E specifies the character encoding for the archive. If not set the database's encoding is used.

The -n switch is used to dump the named schema only. It's possible to specify multiple -n switches to select many schema or using the wildcards. However despite the efforts of pg_dump to get all the dependencies resolved, something could be missing. There's no guarantee the resulting archive can be successfully restored.

The -N switch does the opposite of the -n switch. Excludes the named database schema from the backup. The switch accepts wildcards and it's possible to specify multiple schema with multiple -N switches. When both -n and -N are given, the behaviour is to dump just the schema that match at least one -n switch but no -N switches.

The -o switch option dumps the object id as part of the table for every table. This options should be used only if the OIDs are part of the design.

The -O switch have effects only on plain text exports and does not dump statements setting object ownership.

The -s switch option dumps only the database schema.

The -S switch is meaningful only for plain text exports. The switch specifies the super user for disabling and enabling the triggers if the export is performed with the option –disable-triggers.

The -t switch is used to dump the named table only. It's possible to specify multiple tables using the wildcards or specifying the -t many times.

The -T skips the named table in the dump. It's possible to exclude multiple tables using the wildcards or specifying the -T many times.

The switch -x does not save the grant/revoke commands for setting the privileges.

The switch –binary-upgrade is used only for the in place upgrade program pg_upgrade. Is not intended for general usage.
The switch –insert option dumps the data as INSERT command instead of the COPY. The restore with this option is very slow because each statement is parsed and executed individually.

The switch –column-inserts results in the data exported as INSERT commands with all the column names specified.

The switch –disable-dollar-quoting disables the dollar quoting for the function's body and uses the standard SQL quoting.

The switch –disable-triggers save the statements for disabling the triggers before the data load and the enabling them back after the data load. Disabling the triggers will ensure the foreign keys will not cause errors during the data load. This switch have effect only for the plain text export.

The switch –exclude-table-data=TABLE skips the data dump for the named table. The same rules of the -t and -T apply to this switch.

The switch –no-security-labels doesn't include the security labels into the dump file.

The switch –no-synchronized-snapshots is used to run a parallel export with the pre 9.2 databases. Because the snapshot export feature is missing this means the database shall not change state until all the exporting jobs are connected.

The switch –no-tablespaces skips the tablespace assignments.

The switch –no-unlogged-table-data does not export data for the unlogged relations.

The switch –quote-all-identifiers cause all the identifiers to be enclosed in double quotes.

The switch –section option specifies one of the three export's sections. The first section is the pre-data, which saves the definitions for the tables, the views and the functions. The second section is the data which saves the table's contents. The third section is the post-data which saves the constraints, the indices and the eventual GRANT REVOKE commands . This switch applies only to the plain format.

The switch –serializable-deferrable uses a serializable transaction for the dump, to ensure the database state is consistent. The dump execution waits for a point in the transaction stream without anomalies to avoid the risk of serialization_failure. The option is not useful for the backup used only for disaster recovery and should be used only when the dump should reload into a read only database which needs to get a consistent state compatible with the origin's database.

The switch –use-set-session-authorization sets the objects ownership using the command SET SESSION AUTHORIZATION instead of the ALTER OWNER. SET SESSION AU-THORIZATION requires the super user privileges whereas ALTER OWNER doesn't.

9.2 Performance tips

pg_dump is designed to have a minimal impact on the running cluster. However, any DDL on the saved relations is blocked until the backup' end. VACUUM is less effective when the backup is in progress because the dead rows generated meanwhile pg_dump is running, cannot be freed, because still required by the dump's transaction.

9.2.1 Avoid remote backups

The pg_dump can connect to remote databases like any other PostgreSQL client. It seems reasonable then to use the program installed on a centralised storage and to dump locally from the remote cluster. Unfortunately even using the compressed format, the entire database flows uncompressed over the network from the database server to the remote pg_dump re-ceiver because the compression is done by the receiver.

A far better approach is to save locally the database and then copy the entire dump file using remote copy program like rsync or scp.

9.2.2 Skip replicated tables

If the database is configured as logical slave, backing up the replicated table's data is not important as the contents are re synchronised from the master when the node is re attached to the replication system. The switch –exclude-table-data=TABLE is then useful for dumping just the table's definition without the contents.

9.2.3 Check for slow cpu cores

PostgreSQL is not multi threaded. Each backend is attached to just one cpu core. When pg_dump starts it opens one backend on the cluster which is used to export the database objects. The pg_dump process receives the data output from the backend saving in the chosen format. The single cpu's speed is then critical to avoid a bottleneck. The recently introduced parallel export, implemented with the snapshot exports can improve sensibly the pg_dump performance.

9.2.4 Check for the available locks

PostgreSQL uses the locks in order to enforce the schema and data consistency. For example, when a table is accessed for reading, then an access share lock is set preventing any structure change. The locks on the relations are stored into the pg_locks table. This table is quite unique because have a limited amount of rows determined with the formula.
$$max_locks_per_transaction * (max_connections + max_prepared_transactions)$$

The default settings allow just 6400 lock slots. This value is generally OK. However, if the database have complex schema with hundreds of relations, the backup can exhaust the available slots and fail with an out of memory error. Adjusting the parameters involved in the compute of locks resolve the problem but this requires a cluster restart.

9.3 pg_dump under the bonnet

The pg_dump source code gives a very good picture of what pg_dump does.

The first thing the process does is setting the correct transaction's isolation level. Each server's version requires a different isolation level.

PostgreSQL up to the version 9.0 implements a soft SERIALIZABLE isolation which worked more like the REPETABLE READ. From the version 9.1 the SERIALIZABLE isolation level becomes strict. The strictiest level SERIALIZABLE is used with DEFERRABLE option only when pg_dump is executed with the option –serializable-deferrable The switch have effect only on the remote server with version 9.1 and later though. The transaction is also set to READ ONLY, when supported by the server, in order to reduce the XID generation.

Server version	Command
>= 9.1	REPEATABLE READ, READ ONLY
>= 9.1 with –serializable-deferrable	SERIALIZABLE, READ ONLY, DEFERRABLE
>= 7.4	SERIALIZABLE READ ONLY
<7.4	SERIALIZABLE

Table 9.1: pg_dump's transaction isolation levels

From the version 9.3 pg_dump supports also the parallel dump using the feature seen in 5.8.1. The snapshot export is also supported in the version 9.2 which offers this improvement on the previous version as well. However, using the option –no-synchronized-snapshots tells pg_dump to not issue a snapshot export. This allows a parallel backup from the versions without the snapshot exports. In order to have the data export consistent the database should stop the write operations for the time required to all the export processes to connect.

The parallel dump is available only with the directory format. The pg_restore program from the version 9.3 can do a paralell restore with the directory format as well.

9.4   pg_dumpall

pg_dumpall does not have all the pg_dump's options. The program basically dumps all the cluster's databases in plain format.

However, pg_dumpall is very useful because the switch –globals-only . With this option pg_dumpall saves the the global object definitions in plain text.

This includes the tablespace definitions, the users which are saved with their passwords.

The following example shows the program's execution and the contents of the output file.

```
postgres@tardis:~/dmp$ pg_dumpall --globals-only -f main_globals.sql
postgres@tardis:~/dmp$ cat main_globals.sql
--
-- PostgreSQL database cluster dump
--

SET default_transaction_read_only = off;

SET client_encoding = 'UTF8';
SET standard_conforming_strings = on;


--
-- Roles
--

CREATE ROLE postgres;
ALTER ROLE postgres WITH SUPERUSER INHERIT CREATEROLE CREATEDB LOGIN
    REPLICATION;


--
-- PostgreSQL database cluster dump complete
--

postgres@tardis:~/dmp
```

9.5 Backup validation

There's little advantage in having a backup if this is not valid. The corruption can happen at various levels and unfortunately when the problem is detected is too late.

A corrupted filesystem an hardware problem or a network issue can result in an invalid dump archive.

The filesystem of choice should be solid and with a reliable journal. The disk subsystem should guarantee the data reliability rather the speed. The network interface and the connections should be efficient and capable of handling the transfer without problems. Using the md5 checksum over the archive file is a good technique to check the file's integrity after the transfer.

Obviously this don't give us the certain the backup can be restore. It's important then running a periodical check for the restore. The strategy to use is determined by the amount of data, the time required for the restore and the backup schedule.

The general purpose databases, which size is measurable in hundreds of gigabytes, the restore can complete in few hours and the continuous test is feasible. For the VLDB, which size is measured in terabytes, the restore can take more than one day, in particular if there are big indices requiring expensive sort on disk for the build. In this case a test on a weekly basis is more feasible.

Chapter 10

Restore

There's little advantage in saving the data if the restore is not possible. In this chapter we'll take a look to the fastest and possibly the safest way to restore the saved dump.

The program used for the restore is determined by the dump format. We'll first take a look to the restore using a plain format then the custom and the directory formats. Finally we'll the way to improve the restore performances with a temporary sacrifice of the cluster's reliability.

10.1 The plain format

As seen in 9 the pg_dump's output is plain SQL. The generated script gives no choice but loading it into psql. The SQL statements are parsed and executed in sequence.

This format have few advantages. For example it's possible to edit the statements using a common text editor. This of course if the dump is reasonably small. Even loading a file with vim when its size is measured in gigabytes becomes a stressful experience though.

The data contents are saved using the COPY command. At restore time this choice have the best performance.

It's possible to save the data contents using the inserts. The restore is indeed very slow because each statement has to be parsed, planned and executed.

If the backup saves the schema and the data in two separate files this requires extra care at dump time if there are triggers and foreign keys in the database schema.

The data only backup should include the switch --disable-triggers which writes emit the DISABLE TRIGGER statements before the data load and the ENABLE TRIGGER after the data is restored.

The following example shows a dump/reload session using the separate schema and data dump files.

Let's create a new database with a simple data structure. Two tables storing a city and the address and a foreign key between them enforcing the referential integrity.

```
postgres=# CREATE DATABASE db_addr;
CREATE DATABASE
postgres=# \c db_addr
You are now connected to database "db_addr" as user "postgres".
db_addr=# CREATE TABLE t_address
        (
                i_id_addr serial,
                i_id_city integer NOT NULL,
                t_addr text,
                CONSTRAINT pk_id_address PRIMARY KEY (i_id_addr)
        )
;
CREATE TABLE
db_addr=# CREATE TABLE t_city
        (
                i_id_city        serial,
                v_city           character varying (255),
                v_postcode       character varying (20),
                CONSTRAINT pk_i_id_city PRIMARY KEY (i_id_city)
        )
;
CREATE TABLE
db_addr=# ALTER TABLE t_address ADD
        CONSTRAINT fk_t_city_i_id_city FOREIGN KEY (i_id_city)
        REFERENCES t_city(i_id_city)
          ON DELETE CASCADE
          ON UPDATE RESTRICT;
ALTER TABLE
```

Now let's put some data into the tables.

```
INSERT INTO t_city
        (
          v_city,
          v_postcode
        )
      VALUES
        (
          'Leicester - Stoneygate',
          'LE2 2BH'
        )
      RETURNING i_id_city
;

 i_id_city
-----------
         3
(1 row)

db_addr=# INSERT INTO t_address
        (
```

110

```
                i_id_city,
                t_addr
            )
        VALUES
            (
              3,
              '4, malvern road '
            )
        RETURNING i_id_addr
;

 i_id_addr
-----------
         1
(1 row)
```

We'll now execute dump the schema and the data in two separate plain files. Please note we are not using the –disable-triggers switch.

```
postgres@tardis:~/dmp$ pg_dump --schema-only db_addr > db_addr.schema.sql
postgres@tardis:~/dmp$ pg_dump --data-only db_addr > db_addr.data.sql
```

Looking to the schema dump it's quite obvious what it does. All the DDL are saved in the correct order to restore the same database structure .
The data is then saved by pg_dump in the correct order for having the referential integrity guaranteed. In our very simple example the table t_city is dumped before the table t_address. This way the data will not violate the foreign key. In a complex scenario where multiple foreign keys are referring the same table, the referential order is not guaranteed. Let's run the same dump with the option –disable-trigger.

```
postgres@tardis:~/dmp$ pg_dump --disable-triggers --data-only db_addr > db_addr.data.sql
```

The copy statements in this case are enclosed by two extra statements which disable and then re enable the triggers.

```
ALTER TABLE t_address DISABLE TRIGGER ALL;

COPY t_address (i_id_addr, i_id_city, t_addr) FROM stdin;
1       3       4, malvern road
\.

ALTER TABLE t_address ENABLE TRIGGER ALL;
```

The foreign keys and all the user defined trigger will not fire during the data restore, ensuring the data will be safely stored and improving the speed.

Let's then create a new database where we'll restore the dump starting from the saved schema.

111

```
postgres=# CREATE DATABASE db_addr_restore;
CREATE DATABASE
postgres=# \c db_addr_restore
You are now connected to database "db_addr_restore" as user "postgres".
db_addr_restore=# \i db_addr.schema.sql
SET
...
SET
CREATE EXTENSION
COMMENT
SET
SET
CREATE TABLE
ALTER TABLE
CREATE SEQUENCE
ALTER TABLE
ALTER SEQUENCE
CREATE TABLE
ALTER TABLE
CREATE SEQUENCE
ALTER TABLE
ALTER SEQUENCE
ALTER TABLE
...
ALTER TABLE
REVOKE
REVOKE
GRANT
GRANT
db_addr_restore=# \i db_addr.data.sql
SET
...
SET
ALTER TABLE
...
ALTER TABLE
 setval
--------
      1
(1 row)

 setval
--------
      3
(1 row)

db_addr_restore=# \d
                  List of relations
 Schema |          Name          |   Type   |  Owner
--------+------------------------+----------+----------
 public | t_address              | table    | postgres
 public | t_address_i_id_addr_seq | sequence | postgres
 public | t_city                 | table    | postgres
 public | t_city_i_id_city_seq   | sequence | postgres
(4 rows)
```

10.2 The binary formats

The three binary formats supported by pg_dump are the custom, the directory and the tar format. The first two support the selective access when restoring and the parallel execution. Those features make them the best choice for a flexible and reliable backup. Before the the 9.3 the only format supporting the parallel restore was the custom format. The latest version extended the functionality to the directory format which, combined with the parallel dump improves massively the recovery performances on big amount of data. The tar format which its limitations is suitable for saving only small amount of data.

The custom format is a binary archive. It have a table of contents which can address the the data saved inside the archive. The directory format is composed by toc.dat file where the schema is stored alongside with the references to the zip files where the table's contents are saved. For each table there is a gz mapped inside the toc. Each file contains command, COPY or inserts, for reloading the data in the specific table.

The restore from the binary happens via the pg_restore program which have almost the same switches as pg_dump's as seen in 9.1. This is the pg_restore's help output.

```
pg_restore restores a PostgreSQL database from an archive created by pg_dump.

Usage:
  pg_restore [OPTION]... [FILE]

General options:
  -d, --dbname=NAME        connect to database name
  -f, --file=FILENAME      output file name
  -F, --format=c|d|t       backup file format (should be automatic)
  -l, --list               print summarized TOC of the archive
  -v, --verbose            verbose mode
  -V, --version            output version information, then exit
  -?, --help               show this help, then exit

Options controlling the restore:
  -a, --data-only          restore only the data, no schema
  -c, --clean              clean (drop) database objects before recreating
  -C, --create             create the target database
  -e, --exit-on-error      exit on error, default is to continue
  -I, --index=NAME         restore named index
  -j, --jobs=NUM           use this many parallel jobs to restore
  -L, --use-list=FILENAME  use table of contents from this file for
                           selecting/ordering output
  -n, --schema=NAME        restore only objects in this schema
```

```
-O, --no-owner                  skip restoration of object ownership
-P, --function=NAME(args)       restore named function
-s, --schema-only               restore only the schema, no data
-S, --superuser=NAME            superuser user name to use for disabling triggers
-t, --table=NAME                restore named table(s)
-T, --trigger=NAME              restore named trigger
-x, --no-privileges             skip restoration of access privileges (grant/revoke)
-1, --single-transaction        restore as a single transaction
--disable-triggers              disable triggers during data-only restore
--no-data-for-failed-tables     do not restore data of tables that could not be
                                created
--no-security-labels            do not restore security labels
--no-tablespaces                do not restore tablespace assignments
--section=SECTION               restore named section (pre-data, data, or post-data)
--use-set-session-authorization
                                use SET SESSION AUTHORIZATION commands instead of
                                ALTER OWNER commands to set ownership

Connection options:
-h, --host=HOSTNAME             database server host or socket directory
-p, --port=PORT                 database server port number
-U, --username=NAME             connect as specified database user
-w, --no-password               never prompt for password
-W, --password                  force password prompt (should happen automatically)
--role=ROLENAME                 do SET ROLE before restore
```

If no input file name is supplied, then standard input is used.

Report bugs to <pgsql-bugs@postgresql.org>.

pg_restore requires a file to process and an optional database connection. If the latter is omitted the output is sent to the standard output. However, the switch -f specifies a file where to send the output instead of the standard output. This is very useful if we want just check the original dump file can be read, for example, redirecting the output to /dev/null.

The speed of a restoring from custom or directory, using a database connection, can be massively improved on a multi core system with the -j switch which specifies the number of parallel jobs to run when restoring the data and the post data section.

As said before PostgreSQL does not supports the multithreading. Therefore each parallel job will use just only one cpu over a list of obects to restore determined when pg_resotore is started.

The switch –section works the same way as for pg_dump controlling the section of the archived data to restore. The custom and directory format have these sections.

- **pre-data** This section contains the schema definitions without the keys, indices and triggers.

- **data** This section contains the tables's data contents.

- **post-data** This section contains the objects enforcing the data integrity alongside with the triggers and the indices.

The switch -C is used to create the target database before starting the restore. The connections need also a generic database to connect in order to create the database listed in the archive.

The following example shows the restore of the database created in 10.1 using the custom format, using the schema and the data restore.

First we'll do a pg_dump in custom format.

```
$ pg_dump -Fc -f db_addr.dmp  db_addr
pg_dump: reading schemas
pg_dump: reading user-defined tables
pg_dump: reading extensions
pg_dump: reading user-defined functions
pg_dump: reading user-defined types
pg_dump: reading procedural languages
pg_dump: reading user-defined aggregate functions
pg_dump: reading user-defined operators
pg_dump: reading user-defined operator classes
pg_dump: reading user-defined operator families
pg_dump: reading user-defined text search parsers
pg_dump: reading user-defined text search templates
pg_dump: reading user-defined text search dictionaries
pg_dump: reading user-defined text search configurations
pg_dump: reading user-defined foreign-data wrappers
pg_dump: reading user-defined foreign servers
pg_dump: reading default privileges
pg_dump: reading user-defined collations
pg_dump: reading user-defined conversions
pg_dump: reading type casts
pg_dump: reading table inheritance information
pg_dump: reading event triggers
pg_dump: finding extension members
pg_dump: finding inheritance relationships
pg_dump: reading column info for interesting tables
```

```
pg_dump: finding the columns and types of table "t_address"
pg_dump: finding default expressions of table "t_address"
pg_dump: finding the columns and types of table "t_city"
pg_dump: finding default expressions of table "t_city"
pg_dump: flagging inherited columns in subtables
pg_dump: reading indexes
pg_dump: reading indexes for table "t_address"
pg_dump: reading indexes for table "t_city"
pg_dump: reading constraints
pg_dump: reading foreign key constraints for table "t_address"
pg_dump: reading foreign key constraints for table "t_city"
pg_dump: reading triggers
pg_dump: reading triggers for table "t_address"
pg_dump: reading triggers for table "t_city"
pg_dump: reading rewrite rules
pg_dump: reading large objects
pg_dump: reading dependency data
pg_dump: saving encoding = UTF8
pg_dump: saving standard_conforming_strings = on
pg_dump: saving database definition
pg_dump: dumping contents of table t_address
pg_dump: dumping contents of table t_city
```

We'll then create a new database for restoring the archive.

```
postgres=# CREATE DATABASE db_addr_restore_bin;
CREATE DATABASE
```

The schema restore is done with using the following command.

```
$ pg_restore -v -s -d db_addr_restore_bin db_addr.dmp
pg_restore: connecting to database for restore
pg_restore: creating SCHEMA public
pg_restore: creating COMMENT SCHEMA public
pg_restore: creating EXTENSION plpgsql
pg_restore: creating COMMENT EXTENSION plpgsql
pg_restore: creating TABLE t_address
pg_restore: creating SEQUENCE t_address_i_id_addr_seq
pg_restore: creating SEQUENCE OWNED BY t_address_i_id_addr_seq
pg_restore: creating TABLE t_city
pg_restore: creating SEQUENCE t_city_i_id_city_seq
pg_restore: creating SEQUENCE OWNED BY t_city_i_id_city_seq
pg_restore: creating DEFAULT i_id_addr
pg_restore: creating DEFAULT i_id_city
pg_restore: creating CONSTRAINT pk_i_id_city
```

```
pg_restore: creating CONSTRAINT pk_id_address
pg_restore: creating FK CONSTRAINT fk_t_city_i_id_city
pg_restore: setting owner and privileges for DATABASE db_addr
pg_restore: setting owner and privileges for SCHEMA public
pg_restore: setting owner and privileges for COMMENT SCHEMA public
pg_restore: setting owner and privileges for ACL public
pg_restore: setting owner and privileges for EXTENSION plpgsql
pg_restore: setting owner and privileges for COMMENT EXTENSION plpgsql
pg_restore: setting owner and privileges for TABLE t_address
pg_restore: setting owner and privileges for SEQUENCE t_address_i_id_addr_seq
pg_restore: setting owner and privileges for SEQUENCE OWNED BY t_address_i_id_addr_seq
pg_restore: setting owner and privileges for TABLE t_city
pg_restore: setting owner and privileges for SEQUENCE t_city_i_id_city_seq
pg_restore: setting owner and privileges for SEQUENCE OWNED BY t_city_i_id_city_seq
pg_restore: setting owner and privileges for DEFAULT i_id_addr
pg_restore: setting owner and privileges for DEFAULT i_id_city
pg_restore: setting owner and privileges for CONSTRAINT pk_i_id_city
pg_restore: setting owner and privileges for CONSTRAINT pk_id_address
pg_restore: setting owner and privileges for FK CONSTRAINT fk_t_city_i_id_city
```

The dump file is specified as last parameter. The -d switch tells pg_restore in which database restore the archive. Because we are connecting locally and with the postgres os user, there is no need to specify the authentication parameters.

Then we are ready to load the data. We'll disable again the triggers in order to avoid potential data load failures as seen in 10.1.

```
$ pg_restore --disable-triggers -v -a -d db_addr_restore_bin db_addr.dmp
pg_restore: connecting to database for restore
pg_restore: disabling triggers for t_address
pg_restore: processing data for table "t_address"
pg_restore: enabling triggers for t_address
pg_restore: executing SEQUENCE SET t_address_i_id_addr_seq
pg_restore: disabling triggers for t_city
pg_restore: processing data for table "t_city"
pg_restore: enabling triggers for t_city
pg_restore: executing SEQUENCE SET t_city_i_id_city_seq
pg_restore: setting owner and privileges for TABLE DATA t_address
pg_restore: setting owner and privileges for SEQUENCE SET t_address_i_id_addr_seq
pg_restore: setting owner and privileges for TABLE DATA t_city
pg_restore: setting owner and privileges for SEQUENCE SET t_city_i_id_city_seq
```

The problem with this approach is the presence of the indices when loading the data which is a massive bottleneck. Using the –section instead of the schema and data reload improves the restore performance.

The pre-data section will restore just the bare relations.

```
$ pg_restore --section=pre-data -v  -d db_addr_restore_bin db_addr.dmp
pg_restore: connecting to database for restore
pg_restore: creating SCHEMA public
pg_restore: creating COMMENT SCHEMA public
pg_restore: creating EXTENSION plpgsql
pg_restore: creating COMMENT EXTENSION plpgsql
pg_restore: creating TABLE t_address
pg_restore: creating SEQUENCE t_address_i_id_addr_seq
pg_restore: creating SEQUENCE OWNED BY t_address_i_id_addr_seq
pg_restore: creating TABLE t_city
pg_restore: creating SEQUENCE t_city_i_id_city_seq
pg_restore: creating SEQUENCE OWNED BY t_city_i_id_city_seq
pg_restore: creating DEFAULT i_id_addr
pg_restore: creating DEFAULT i_id_city
pg_restore: setting owner and privileges for DATABASE db_addr
pg_restore: setting owner and privileges for SCHEMA public
pg_restore: setting owner and privileges for COMMENT SCHEMA public
pg_restore: setting owner and privileges for ACL public
pg_restore: setting owner and privileges for EXTENSION plpgsql
pg_restore: setting owner and privileges for COMMENT EXTENSION plpgsql
pg_restore: setting owner and privileges for TABLE t_address
pg_restore: setting owner and privileges for SEQUENCE t_address_i_id_addr_seq
pg_restore: setting owner and privileges for SEQUENCE OWNED BY t_address_i_id_addr_se
pg_restore: setting owner and privileges for TABLE t_city
pg_restore: setting owner and privileges for SEQUENCE t_city_i_id_city_seq
pg_restore: setting owner and privileges for SEQUENCE OWNED BY t_city_i_id_city_seq
pg_restore: setting owner and privileges for DEFAULT i_id_addr
pg_restore: setting owner and privileges for DEFAULT i_id_city
```

The data section will then load the data contents as fast as possible.

```
$ pg_restore --section=data -v  -d db_addr_restore_bin db_addr.dmp
pg_restore: connecting to database for restore
pg_restore: implied data-only restore
pg_restore: processing data for table "t_address"
pg_restore: executing SEQUENCE SET t_address_i_id_addr_seq
pg_restore: processing data for table "t_city"
pg_restore: executing SEQUENCE SET t_city_i_id_city_seq
pg_restore: setting owner and privileges for TABLE DATA t_address
```

```
pg_restore: setting owner and privileges for SEQUENCE SET t_address_i_id_addr_seq
pg_restore: setting owner and privileges for TABLE DATA t_city
pg_restore: setting owner and privileges for SEQUENCE SET t_city_i_id_city_seq
```

Finally, the post-data section will create the constraint and the indices over the existig data.

```
$ pg_restore --section=post-data -v  -d db_addr_restore_bin db_addr.dmp
pg_restore: connecting to database for restore
pg_restore: creating CONSTRAINT pk_i_id_city
pg_restore: creating CONSTRAINT pk_id_address
pg_restore: creating FK CONSTRAINT fk_t_city_i_id_city
pg_restore: setting owner and privileges for CONSTRAINT pk_i_id_city
pg_restore: setting owner and privileges for CONSTRAINT pk_id_address
pg_restore: setting owner and privileges for FK CONSTRAINT fk_t_city_i_id_city
```

10.3   Restore performances

When the disaster happens the main goal is to get the database up and running as fast as possible. Usually the data section's restore, if saved with the COPY is usually fast.

The bottleneck is the post-data section which requires CPU intensive operations with random disk access operations. In large databases this section can require more time than the entire data section even if the objects built by the post-data section are smaller. The parallel can improve the speed but sometimes is not enough.

The postgresql.conf file can be tweaked in order to improve dramatically restore's speed up to the 40% compared to production's configuration. This is possible because the restore configuration disables some settings used by PostgreSQL to guarantee the durability. The emergency configuration must be swapped with the production settings as soon as the restore is complete to avoid a further data loss. What follows assumes the production's database is lost and restore is reading from a custom format's backup.

10.3.1   shared_buffers

When Bulk load operations like reloading a big amount of data into the database generates an high eviction rate from the shared buffer without caching. Reducing the size of the shared buffer will not affect the load. Therefore more memory will be available for the backends when processing the post-data section. There's no fixed rule for the sizing. A gross approximation could at least 10 MB for each parallel job with a minimum shared buffer's size of 512 MB.

10.3.2   wal_level

The parameter wal_level sets the amount of redo records to store in the WAL segments. By default is the value is to minimal which is used for the standalone clusters. If the cluster feeds a standby server or there is a the point in time recovery setup, the wal_level must be at least archive or hot_standby. If there is a PITR or a standby server available for the recover stop reading this book and act immediately. Restoring from a physical backup is several time faster rather a logical restore. Otherwise, the standby or PITR snapshot is lost as well, before starting the reload the wal_level must be set to minimal to reduce the WAL generation rate.

10.3.3   fsync

Turning off fsync can improve the restore's speed. Unless there is a backup battery on the disk cache, turning off this parameter in production is not safe and can lead to data loss in case of power failure.

10.3.4   checkpoint_segments, checkpoint_timeout

The checkpoint is a periodic event in the database activity. When occurs all the dirty pages in the shared buffer are synced to disk. This can interfere with the restore's bulk operations. Increasing the checkpoint segments and the checkpoint timeout to the maximum allowed will limit the unnecessary IO caused by the frequent checkpoints.

10.3.5   autovacuum

Turning off the autovacuum will avoid to have the tables meanwhile are restored reducing the unnecessary IO.

10.3.6   max_connections

Reducing the max connections to the number of restore jobs plus an extra headroom of five connections will limit the memory consumption caused by the unused memory slots.

10.3.7   port and listen_addresses

When the database is restoring nobody except pg_restore and the DBA should connect it. Changing the port to a different value and disabling the listen addresses except the localhost is a quick and easy solution to avoid the users messing up with the restore process.

10.3.8   maintenance_work_memory

This parameter affects the post-data section's speed. With low values the backends will sort the data on disk slowing down the restore. Higher values will build the new indices in memory improving the speed. However the value's size should be set keeping in mind how much ram is available on the system. This value should be reduced by a 20% if the total ram lesser than to 10 GB. For bigger amount of memory the reduction should be the 10%. This will leave out from the estimate the memory consumed by the operating system and the other processes. From the remaining memory ram scould be removed the the shared_buffer's memory. Finally the remaining value must be divided by the max connections.

Let's consider a a system with 26GB ram. If we set the shared_buffer to 2 GB and 10 max connections, the maintenance_work_mem will be 2.14 GB.

```
26 - 10% =  23.4
23.4 - 2 = 21.4
21.4 / 10 = 2.14
```

Chapter 11

A couple of things to know before start coding...

This chapter is to the developers approaching the PostgreSQL universe. PostgreSQL is a fantastic infrastructure for building powerful and applications. In order to use it at its best, some things to consider. In particular some subtle caveats can make the difference between a magnificent success or a miserable failure.

11.1 SQL is your friend

Recently the rise of the NOSQL engines, has shown more than ever how SQL is a fundamental requirement for managing the data efficiently. Shortcuts to the solution, like the ORMs sooner or later will show their limits. Despite the bad reputation the SQL language is very simple to understand, with few English keywords and a powerful structured syntax which interacts perfectly with the regulated database layer. This simplicity have a cost. The language is parsed and converted into the database's structure causing sometimes misunderstanding between developer requests and the database results.

Mastering the SQL is a slow and difficult process and requires some sort of empathy with the DBMS. Asking for advice to the database administrator when building any design is a good idea to have a better understanding of what the database thinks. Having a few words with the DBA is a good idea in any case though.

11.2 The design comes first

One of the worst mistakes when building an application is to forget about the foundation, the database. With the rise of the ORM[1] this is happening more frequently than it could be

---

[1] Yes, I hate the ORMs

expected. Sometimes the database itself is considered just storage, a big mistake.

The database design is either a complex and important and too much delicate to make it using by a dumb automatic tool. For example, using a generic abstraction layer will build access methods that will almost certainly ignore the PostgreSQL peculiar update strategy, resulting in bloat and general poor performance.

It doesn't matter if the database is simple or the project is small. Nobody knows how successful could be a new idea. A robust design will make the project scale properly.

11.3 Clean coding

Writing decently formatted code is something any developer should do. This have a couple of immediate advantages. Improves the code readability when other developers need review it. Makes the code more manageable when, for example, is read months after it was written. This good practice forgets constantly to include the SQL. Is quite common to find long queries written all lowercase on one line with and the keywords used as identifier.

Trying to read such queries is a nightmare. Often it takes more time in reformatting the queries rather doing the performance tuning. The following guidelines are a good reference for writing decent SQL and avoid a massive headache to the DBA.

11.3.1 The identifier's name

Any DBMS have its way of managing the identifiers. PostgreSQL converts all lowercase. This doesn't work very well with the camel case. It's still possible to mix upper and lower case letters enclosing the identifier name between double quotes. But that means the quoting should be put everywhere. Using the underscores instead of the camel case is simpler.

11.3.2 Self explaining schema

When a database structure becomes complex is very difficult to say what is what and how relates with the other objects. A design diagram or a data dictionary can help. But they can be outdated or not available. Using a simple notation to add to the relation's name will give an immediate outlook of the object's kind.

Object	Prefix
Table	t_
View	v_
Btree Index	idx_bt_
GiST Index	idx_gst_
GIN Index	idx_gin_
Unique index	u_idx_
Primary key	pk_
Foreign key	fk_
Check	chk_
Unique key	uk_
Type	ty_
Sql function	fn_sql_
PlPgsql function	fn_plpg_
PlPython function	fn_plpy_
PlPerl function	fn_plpr_
Trigger	trg_
rule	rul_

A similar approach can be used for the column names, making the data type immediately recognisable.

Type	Prefix
Character	c_
Character varying	v_
Integer	i_
Text	t_
Bytea	by_
Numeric	n_
Timestamp	ts_
Date	d_
Double precision	dp_
Hstore	hs_
Custom data type	ty_

11.3.3 Query formatting

Having a properly formatted query helps to understand which objects are involved in the request and their relations. Even a simple query can be difficult to understand if badly written.

```
select * from debitnoteshead a join debitnoteslines b on debnotid
where a.datnot=b. datnot and b.deblin>1;
```

Let's list the query's issues.

- using lowercase keywords it makes difficult to distinguish them from the identifiers

- the wildcard * mask which fields are really needed; returning all the fields consumes more bandwidth than required; it prevents the index only scans

- the meaningless aliases like *a* and *b* are confusing the query's logic

- without proper indention the query logic cannot be understood

Despite existence of tools capable to prettify such queries, their usage doesn't solve the root problem. Writing decently formatted SQL helps to create a mental map of what the query should removing as well the confusion when building the SQL.

The following rules should be kept in mind constantly when writing SQL.

- All SQL keywords should be in upper case

- All the identifiers and keywords should be grouped at same indention level and separated with a line break

- In the SELECT list avoid the wildcard *

- Specify explicitly the join method in order to make it clear the query's logic

- Adopt meaningful aliases

This is the prettified query.

```
SELECT
        productcode,
        noteid,
        datnot
FROM
        debitnoteshead head
        INNER JOIN
                debitnoteslines lines
                ON
                                head.debnotid=lines.debnotid
                AND             head.datnot=lines.datnot
WHERE
                lines.deblin>1
;
```

11.4   Get DBA advice

The database administration is weird. It's very difficult to explain what a DBA does. It's a job where the statement "failure is not an option" is the rule number zero. A DBA usually works in antisocial hours, with a very tight time schedule.

126

Despite the strange reputation, a database expert is an incredible resource for building up efficient designs. Nowadays is very simple to set up a PostgreSQL cluster. Even with the default configuration the system is so efficient that under normal load doesn't show any problem. This could look like a fantastic feature but actually is a really bad thing. Any mistake at design level is hidden and when the problem appears is maybe too late to fix it.

This final advice is probably the most important of the entire chapter. If you have a DBA don't be shy. Ask for any suggestion, even if the solution seems obvious or if the design seems simple. The database layer is a universe full of pitfalls where a small mistake can result in a very big problem.

Of course if there's no DBA, that's bad. Never sail without a compass. Never start a database project without an expert's advice. Somebody to look after of the most important part of the business, the foundations.

Appendix A

Versioning and support policy

The PostgreSQL version's number is composed by three integer. The first number is the generational version. Currently the value is 9. This number changes when there is a substantial generational gap with the previous version. For example the version 9.0 started its life as 8.5. Later was decided the change of generation.

The second number is the major version. The value starts from zero and increases by one for each release along the generation. Because each major version differs internally from the others the data area is not compatible between them. Usually a new major version is released on a yearly basis.

The third number is the minor version. Usually a new minor release appears when a sufficient number of bug fixes are merged into the codebase. Upgrading a minor version usually requires just the binary upgrade and the cluster restart. However is a good practice to check for any extra action required in the release notes.

The PostgreSQL project aims to fully support a major release for five years. The policy is applied on a best-effort basis.

Version	Supported	First release date	End of life date
9.4	Yes	December 2014	December 2019
9.3	Yes	September 2013	September 2018
9.2	Yes	September 2012	September 2017
9.1	Yes	September 2011	September 2016
9.0	Yes	September 2010	September 2015
8.4	No	July 2009	July 2014

Table A.1: End Of Life (EOL) dates

Appendix B

PostgreSQL 9.4

The new PostgreSQL major version, the 9.4 was released the 18th of December 2014. Alongside the new developer wise features this release introduces several enhancements making the DBA life easier.

B.1   ALTER SYSTEM

This long waited feature gives the DBA the power to alter the configuration parameters from the SQL client. The parameters are validated when the command is issued. Invalid values are spotted immediately reducing the risk of having an hosed cluster because of syntax errors.

For example, the following command sets the parameter wal_level to hot_standby.

```
ALTER SYSTEM SET wal_level = hot_standby;
```

B.2   autovacuum_work_mem

This setting sets the maintenance work memory only for the autovacuum workers. As seen in 8.1 the vacuum performance is affected by the maintenance_work_mem. This new parameter allows a better flexibility in the automatic vacuum tuning.

B.3   huge_pages

This parameter enables or disables the use of huge memory pages on Linux. Turning on this parameter can result in a reduced CPU usage for managing large amount of memory on Linux.

B.4 Replication Slots

With the replication slots the master becomes aware of the slave's replication status. The master with replication slots allocated does not remove the WAL segments until they have been received by all the standbys. Also the master does not remove the rows which could cause a recovery conflict even when the standby is disconnected.

B.5 Planning time

Now EXPLAIN ANALYZE shows the time spent by the planner to build the execution plan, giving to the performance tuners a better understanding of the query efficiency.

B.6 pg_prewarm

This additional module loads the relation's data into the shared buffer after a shutdown. This allows the cluster reaching the efficiency quickly.

Appendix C

Contacts

- Email: 4thdoctor.gallifrey@gmail.com
- Twitter: @4thdoctor_scarf
- Blog: http://www.pgdba.co.uk

List of Figures

List of Tables

Index

www.ingramcontent.com/pod-product-compliance
Lightning Source LLC
Chambersburg PA
CBHW080422060326
40689CB00019B/4346